A STUDY OF ROMANS

Soul full

E   F

⋙ LIVING OUT A ROBUST FAITH ⋘

DONNA GAINES

MARGE LENOW

JEAN STOCKDALE

DAYNA STREET

Soul-Full: Living Out a Robust Faith

© 2016 Bellevue Baptist Church

Cover and book design: Amanda Weaver

 CONTENTS

⫸ HOW TO USE THIS STUDY ⫷

This ten-week study of Romans is designed to provide an opportunity for individual study throughout the week leading up to a group meeting once a week. Each session is divided into five daily homework assignments and provides Scripture and personal application with room for notes and journaling what you will learn along the way.

Use these notes and what you learn throughout the week to facilitate discussion amongst your group. We encourage you to close your group with a time of prayer.

INTRODUCTION

Welcome to the study of Romans! Romans is truly "the gospel according to Paul." Throughout the course of this study you will come to understand this gospel and how it affects your life today. It is much more than a simple story; it is life-altering truth that causes each of us to have to make a decision upon encountering it.

In this study you will:

- Take up the life in the spirit and live as people of faith.
- Rest in the assurance of God's love, the intercession of our Savior and the help of the Holy Spirit.
- Understand God's gracious provision for our need for salvation.
- Receive and achieve righteousness in Christ by faith.
- Filling up with Faith sections will prepare us for conversations with those outside the faith as we explore basic apologetics that are laced throughout the book of Romans.

The gospel truly is "good news." God demands righteousness, and He provides it on our behalf through His son, Jesus Christ. Through His Spirit we are empowered to obey. May your faith be strengthened and your witness sharpened as we study this most important New Testament book.

WEEK ONE

Unashamed!

For I am not ashamed of the gospel, for it is the power of God for salvation to
everyone who believes, to the Jew first and also to the Greek.
Romans 1:16

Romans 1

Background:

First Century Rome dominated Europe, North Africa, and the Near East. It continued expanding, most notably conquering Britain under the emperor Claudius.

> Rome — the most celebrated city in the world at the time of Christ. It is said to have been founded in 753 BC. When the New Testament was written, Rome was enriched and adorned with the spoils of the world, and contained a population estimated at 1,200,000, of which the half were slaves, and including representatives of nearly every nation then known. It was distinguished for its wealth and luxury and profligacy. The empire of which it was the capital had then reached its greatest prosperity. [1]

Paul had desired to visit Rome (Acts 19:21). This letter is believed to have been written at the end of his third missionary journey around AD 57. Paul probably wrote the letter from Corinth.

Although never having visited the church, Paul felt a connection with these brothers and sisters in Christ. He looked forward to seeing them in person, but until that time, he wrote them to present a thorough statement of faith. He systematically detailed man's lost state and our need of a Savior. Then, stressing that there was no difference between Jew and Gentile, he proclaimed salvation by grace through faith in Christ alone.

Many believe the church at Rome was started by those who had experienced Pentecost.

> Other believers migrated to Rome through the years since Pentecost, for Rome was a magnet that drew people from all over the empire for business and other reasons. Aquila and Priscilla are good examples. They had lived in Italy before (Acts 18:2), and undoubtedly returned as soon as circumstances permitted. Phoebe (Rom. 16:1-2), apparently the courier of this letter, is another example. She did not go to Rome primarily to deliver Paul's letter; she delivered Paul's letter because she was making a trip to Rome. In fact, Phoebe's planned

trip to Rome was undoubtedly the specific occasion for Paul's writing this letter. Humanly speaking, Paul seized this opportunity to communicate with a group of Christians he was deeply interested in and planned to visit as soon as possible."[2]

The gospel is "good news." It is a fact of history, and yet, as current as today's headlines, because "news" is new. If you know Christ, then He is actively at work in your life today. As you launch into this study of God's Word, your faith will get a boost and your hope will be renewed. Thank the Lord as you begin for His love as our Father and for the intercession of our Savior and the help of the Holy Spirit. For it is truly through Him that we overwhelmingly conquer! (Romans 8:37)

⫸ WEEK 1 · DAY ONE ⫷

Romans 1:1-17

1. How does Paul refer to himself? (v.1)

   -

   -

   -

2. What is a bond-slave? (Exodus 21:5-7; Deuteronomy 15:16-18)

   The Lord Jesus Christ loved us and gave Himself for us, but He never makes us His slaves. You must come voluntarily to Him and make yourself His slave.[3]

3. To whom is the book addressed? (vv. 5-7)

4. How was Christ declared the Son of God?

   "You see, the resurrection did not make Him the Son of God; it simply revealed who He was."[4]

5. What does the phrase "the obedience of faith" in verse 5 mean?

6. Faith will always result in obedience. Is there an area of disobedience in your life that is a direct result of lack of faith?

7. Look up these verses and prayerfully consider each:

       Fear — 2 Timothy 1:7

       Worry — Philippians 4:6-7

       Poor financial stewardship — Matthew 6:19-24

       Prayerlessness — Luke 18:1-8

       Unforgiveness — Matthew 18:21-35

       Anger — Ephesians 4:26-27; Matthew 5:21-24

       Bitterness — Ephesians 4:31-32

8. For what is Paul grateful? Why?

Is the resurrection of Jesus true?

Historical proof of the resurrection:

> The bodily resurrection of Christ is the crowning proof that Jesus was who he claimed to be, God manifested in human flesh. Indeed, the resurrection of Christ in flesh is of such importance to the Christian faith that the New Testament insists that no one can be saved without it (Romans 10:9; 1 Corinthians 15:1-7)…The evidence for this is found in his twelve appearances, the first eleven of which cover the immediate forty days after his crucifixion.[5]

Jesus was seen, heard, touched and He even ate in His resurrected body. He appeared to individuals, small groups and even 500 people at one time as recorded in 1 Corinthians 15:6. How would you defend the resurrection to a seeker?

Romans 1:1-17

1. What is Paul's desire?

2. Paul says he is under obligation to preach the gospel. We too are under obligation. We have been given a mandate from our Lord — Matthew 28:19-20. Are you fulfilling His command? How?

3. Romans 1:16-17 has been selected by many as the theme for Romans. How would you paraphrase this theme?

4. How shall we live by faith? (v. 17)

   Faith (believing God) will always be the automatic response of the spirit. But trusting God and venturing out where you cannot see with the eyes of reason, logic, and common sense will always pose a struggle for the flesh.[6]

5. Define faith according to the Bible. (Include scripture references.)

6. Write out your own definition of faith. (Paraphrase Romans 1:16-17.)

Without faith it is impossible to please God. Hebrews 11:6a

Romans 1:18-32

Not only is the righteousness of God revealed, but the fallenness of man is evident as well. We need only read the newspaper or turn on the television to see evidence of man's unrighteousness. Paul is revealing what takes place in society when man turns away from God and God begins to remove the restraining influence of His Spirit. As God removes His hand, we are given over to depraved minds and increased immorality and depravity. If left to our own devices we **will** self-destruct.

1. How is the truth suppressed?

2. How is God made evident?

3. What are the two things ungodly people fail to do? (v. 21)

4. What is the result of a lack of gratitude and thanksgiving?

5. What does the Bible say about wisdom apart from God?

Romans 1:18-32

We know from scripture that seeking wisdom apart from God makes us fools, for our foolish hearts will be darkened as we lean on our own understanding (Romans 1:21-22).

1. Suppressing the truth and elevating our own reasoning above the Word of God leads to what? (vv. 24-32)

2. List evidences of these sins in our society:

3. What needs to happen for a person to acknowledge God and recognize his or her sin?

4. Why does God allow people to be given over to depravity? What good can come as a result? (Hosea 5:15; Amos 4:6-14; 2 Chronicles 7:13-14)

5. How does this affect the way you will evangelize and pray for people?

6. Any time a list of sins is mentioned in scripture, we can be assured that the opposite of these sins should be evident in our lives as believers. Make a list of these positive attributes:

7. What should a Christian do if any of the listed sins are present in his or her life? (1 John 1:8-10)

⫸ FILLING UP WITH FAITH

Does God exist?

There are many people in our post-modern world who claim that they either are skeptical that God exists, they are unsure or completely deny His existence. The following are definitions of these beliefs.

Skepticism – The skeptic doubts that God exists.

Agnosticism – "An agnostic is someone who claims not to know. As applied to knowledge of God, there are two basic kinds of agnostics, those who claim that the existence and nature of God are not known, and those who hold God to be unknowable."[7]

Atheism – An atheist believes that God does not exist. They believe that there is the cosmos and nothing else.

Choose either the skeptic, atheist or agnostic and write down the reasoning you would use to prove the existence of God.

Romans 1:1-32

In the foreword to J. B. Phillips commentary on Romans, Alan Redpath writes:

> After all, what is the value of being forgiven for our sins only to continue living in them? The death of Christ on Calvary is only half the truth; the other half is the saving life of Christ, by His Holy Spirit, reproducing His character and delivering us from the principle of sin. At the cross we have forgiveness for what we have done, in order that we may stop doing it![8]

1. God has repeatedly told His people to choose obedience, thus choosing life. Look up the following verses and record the obedience that leads to blessing.

    Deuteronomy 4:23-30

    Deuteronomy 30:15-20

    Joshua 24:15-24

    Isaiah 1:16-20

    John 12:24-26

    Revelation 3:14-22

But to this one I will look, to him who is humble and contrite of spirit, and who trembles at My word. Isaiah 66:2b

What is truth?

Absolute truth is truth that is true for all people, in all places, at all times. God's Word is true. How would you talk with someone about the truth of God's Word?

What scriptures would you use?

If there is a Creator Who has revealed Himself and His will through His written Word and through His Son, then it stands to reason that He would know how life was designed to work. God's desire is for human flourishing. It is when we reject God's truth that we experience the pain and separation of our own sin. What command of God's Word do you struggle most obeying?

WEEK TWO

The Condemnation of Sin

ROMANS 2-3

Or do you think lightly of the riches of His kindness and tolerance and patience
not knowing that the kindness of God leads you to repentance?
Romans 2:4

In Romans 1:18-32, Paul utilized the third person when he referred to fallen, sinful mankind:

- For even though *they* knew no God (v. 20)
- *They* became futile in *their* speculations (v. 21)
- *Their* foolish heart was hardened (v. 21)
- Professing to be wise, *they* became fools (v. 22)
- *They* exchanged the truth of God for a lie (v. 25)
- God gave *them* over to a depraved mind (v. 28)

At the opening of Romans 2, Paul shifts his address from third person to second person, you, a more direct approach in condemning sin. Commentators refer to Paul's style in this chapter as diatribal. Diatribe was a communication style commonly used at that time. In a diatribe, a writer would debate with his readers by giving voice to his opposition through the form of a question. Once the question was posed, he would then refute his objector's position. As we will see throughout our time in God's Word this week, Paul consistently refutes any argument that someone might pose regarding his or her own personal righteousness, concluding that "all have sinned and fall short of the glory of God." Romans 3:23

>>> DAY ONE <<<

Romans 2:1-16

1. What kind of a response do these verses elicit?

2. How has God written the law in our hearts? (v. 15)

3. Look up Ecclesiastes 3:11. What else has He put in our hearts?

4. What secrets do you have from others that will be exposed before Christ?

Many times these secrets are just the open door the enemy needs to wreak havoc in our lives. If the sin has been confessed to the Lord and forsaken – **you are forgiven!!** If you are still struggling with guilt or battling with your thoughts in this area of sin, you need to find a trusted spiritual friend or mentor with whom you can confess your sin. James 5:16 says, "Confess your sins to each other and pray for each other so that you may be healed. The earnest prayer of a righteous person has great power and wonderful results" (NLT). What you have kept hidden in darkness will no longer have a hold on you, once it is confessed and brought out into the light. Crucify your pride, (remember it goes before a fall) and take action. Declare war on what the enemy has sought to steal from you and begin to walk in the freedom and victory Christ purchased for you on Calvary.

5. Read Hebrews 4:13, James 5:16, and 1 John 1:9. According to these scriptures, how should we deal with hidden sin?

Sylvia Gunter, author of *Prayer Portions,* has said, "The only power the enemy has over a Christian is the power of secrets." How much power have you been giving to the enemy that needs to be taken back? Stop right now and pray. Ask the Lord to show you the action you are to take according to His Word.

Romans 2:17-29

1. If the Spirit of God has circumcised our hearts, and we have been sealed with His Spirit, then it should be evident by how we live. How do we dishonor God with our behavior?

2. Does your personal behavior honor or dishonor God?

3. The Jews were self-righteous, which is pride. Have you ever found yourself looking down on someone else or feeling spiritually superior? What does God say about this? (vv. 17-24)

4. Who are those of the true circumcision? (Galatians 5:6; Philippians 3:1-11)

For several summers, our church put on "Girl Talk" events. Once a month, we'd have a special speaker come in to share with "just us girls" how we can live out the Christian life. We have learned about marriage, parenting, friendship, adversity, the power of our testimony and have been encouraged to be all the Lord has called and created us to be. This ministry evolved into what we call "Girl Walk." Taking the letters of GIRL we created an acrostic: God's Instruction Regarding Life: Walk it, don't just talk it! This is the crux of what Paul is saying to the Romans. It is the same message James recorded in his epistle when he said faith without works is dead. We are not saved *by* works, but works are the evidence that we are saved. When others look at your life, is it evident you belong to Christ? How would your family members describe you? What about your closest friends?

"Christians are just a bunch of hypocrites!"

When the world infiltrates the church and believers begin to value what the world values, we are no longer salt and light. We live in a day when "cultural Christianity" has stolen the power from the church because believers live in such a way that they are not "separate" as scripture commands us to be (see 2 Corinthians 6:17). Examine your own life and ask the Lord to show you any compromises that may be quenching the flow of the Holy Spirit (see 1 Thessalonians 5:19) in your life, thus tarnishing your witness.

Romans 3:1-20

1. The Jews were chosen and entrusted with God's Word – "to whom much is given, much is required" (Luke 12:48). As Christians, we have the complete Word of God. We have even more revelation than the Jews to whom Paul was writing. We, of all people, have been entrusted with much! How are you faithfully giving of what God has entrusted to you?

2. How are you living out what you know? Are you obeying God in the areas that you know His will and Word?

    Your personal walk with Christ

    Your marriage

    With your children

    At church

    At work

    In your neighborhood

    With your friends

    In the community

    In the world

How are you reflecting Christ in each of these areas? On a scale of one to ten with ten being the best, how would you rate yourself?

3. We must admit there are times when we are trying "so hard" to grow in our walk with Christ and yet we can become frustrated with our lack of progress or victory. Are you stuck in the "performance" rut? It may be that you need to take some things off of your "to do" list and focus more of your time and energy on "being" with Christ. Are you relying on the Holy Spirit to do His work in you, or are you relying on self?

4. God is. That irrefutable fact remains whether we believe it or not (v. 3). Because He alone is God, we should submit to Him through obedience to His Word. How has God shown Himself faithful even when you have been unfaithful?

On a trip to Student Leadership University with our high school students, Jay Strack made a profound statement to challenge the students. He said, "I will be the exact same person I am today, five years from now, except for the places I go, the people I meet, the books I read, and what I memorize." Dr. Bill Brown said, "You will never become in the future what you are not becoming today." Most of us desire to be godly women. What are you doing to ensure that you meet that goal? What specific steps are you taking? Write them out. (This will help you take the first steps of action toward meeting your goals.)

Romans 3:21-31

Paul refers to the Law and the Prophets, thus signifying the entire Old Testament points to the righteousness of God through faith in Jesus Christ. There is now no distinction; Jew and Gentile are all "justified as a gift by His grace" (3:24). For truly "all have sinned and fall short of the glory of God" (3:23). The requirement for the forgiveness of sin has always been the shedding of the blood of the innocent on behalf of the guilty. Justification is an act that God performs. There are no degrees of justification — it simply means you are now in right standing with God. Becoming more like Him is the process of sanctification. At the point of salvation you are justified, and God begins to conform you to the image of His Son, which is sanctification.

1. How are we made right in God's sight? (Provide other scripture references.)

Hallelujah!! Salvation is for everyone — we can all be saved — no matter who we are or what we have done! Did you get that? **No matter what** we have done!! Take a moment to thank the Lord for His grace and mercy to you.

2. How does Jesus' death on the cross satisfy God's love and justice?

3. What does the word propitiation mean? (v. 25)

Verse 25 also tells us we are made right through "faith in His blood." Forgiveness has always required a blood sacrifice. Work back through the Old Testament and see how God established this precedent. Begin in Genesis 3 when an animal had to die for Adam and Eve to be clothed after their sin ("For the wages of sin is death" Romans 6:23). Can you trace the scarlet thread through the Old Testament?

Romans 3:13-31

1. What does it mean for God to "pass over" the sins previously committed? Where else have you seen this illustrated in the Old Testament?

2. What does verse 27 say makes us right with God?

If our right standing with God isn't based on our works, do we have anything to boast about? My justification is based on what Christ did for me and is offered to me as a gift from God the Father. Therefore, I am saved by grace, kept by grace and will one day be taken to heaven by grace. It is all of God. I surrender my life to His Holy Spirit that I might live in such a way that I glorify Him and draw others to Him.

3. Redemption is literally the recalling of captives (sinners) from captivity (sin) through the payment of a ransom for them. What is the ransom Christ paid?

Propitiation — According to the Hebrew/Greek Key Word Study Bible propitiation means:

> Mercy seat, the lid or the covering of the Ark of the Covenant made of pure gold, on and before which the high priest was to sprinkle the blood of the expiatory sacrifices on the great day of atonement, and where the Lord promised to meet His people (Exodus 25:17, 22; 29:42; 30:36; Leviticus 16:2, 14, 15). Paul, by applying this title to Christ in Romans 3:25, assures us that Christ was the true mercy seat, the reality of the cover of the Ark of the Covenant (Hebrews 9:5) (page 1842).

4. Why is the meaning of this word significant? How does this knowledge enhance the meaning of propitiation that you defined yesterday in question 3?

5. Does faith nullify the law?

6. Read Romans 3:31 in The Message translation:

> *But by shifting our focus from what we do to what God does, don't we cancel out all our careful keeping of the rules and ways God commanded? Not at all. What happens, in fact, is that by putting that entire way of life in its proper place, we confirm it.*

What shift in focus is He talking about? How does it change the way we live?

WEEK THREE

Righteousness by Faith

ROMANS 4

Yet, with respect to the promise of God, he did not waver in unbelief
but grew strong in faith, giving glory to God.
Romans 4:20

What do you think of when you hear the word *forefather*? Perhaps you think of the founding fathers of our great nation, those brave men who stood on principle and risked everything so that we could live in the freedoms we have today. Maybe you think about someone in your family, an ancestor, someone you have never even met, but whose commitment to Christ, work ethic, and personal choices have marked your family for generations. In Romans 4, we see that Paul traced his heritage all the way back to Abraham. Just as many of us view our parents and grandparents as examples to follow, Paul looked to Abraham as a spiritual role model and points us to him as the standard bearer of faith:

> When everything was hopeless, Abraham believed anyway, deciding to live not on the basis of what he saw he couldn't do but on what God said he would do. And so he was made father of a multitude of peoples. God himself said to him, "You're going to have a big family, Abraham!" Abraham didn't focus on his own impotence and say, "It's hopeless. This hundred-year-old body could never father a child." Nor did he survey Sarah's decades of infertility and give up. He didn't tiptoe around God's promise asking cautiously skeptical questions. He plunged into the promise and came up strong, ready for God, sure that God would make good on what he had said. Romans 4:18-21 (MSG)

⋙ DAY ONE ⋘

Romans 4:1-25

Paul spent the first three chapters describing man's sinful condition and hopelessness apart from Christ. He also stressed our inability to keep the law and save ourselves. In Romans 4, he gives us two examples from the Old Testament of those who were justified by God: Abraham and David.

1. How was Abraham declared righteous? Is this the same as salvation?

2. Read Genesis 15:1-6. What promise did God make to Abraham?

3. Was Abraham justified before or after he was circumcised?

4. Who is Abraham the father of?

5. Abraham took God at His Word. The Bible says he didn't waver. Read James 1:5-8. What does the Bible say about those who doubt?

Romans 4:1-12

1. In Romans 4:6-8, Paul quotes David. David makes two startling statements about God's forgiveness. List them below:

    a.

    b.

    In other words, once we are justified, our record contains Christ's perfect righteousness *and can never again contain our sins.* Christians do sin, and these sins need to be forgiven if we are to have fellowship with God (1 John 1:5–7); *but these sins are not held against us.* God does keep a record of our works, so that He might reward us when Jesus comes; but He is not keeping a record of our sins.[9]

2. The Psalm that is quoted here is Psalm 32. Read it and list the blessings of forgiveness.

3. The righteousness God demands, He also provides. Read 1 Corinthians 1:30 and 2 Corinthians 5:21. Write your own paraphrase of these verses.

Under law, God required righteousness from man. Under grace, He gives righteousness to man.

Romans 4:13-25

1. Abraham's circumstances didn't seem to match the promise of God. But, Abraham believed and then he saw. That is the pattern of God — He requires that we walk by faith and not by sight. Read John 6:27-29. What is the work of God?

2. Who else in Scripture did God call to obey by faith before He granted sight?

3. Read Romans 4:13-14 from The Message:

   That famous promise God gave Abraham — that he and his children would possess the earth — was not given because of something Abraham did or would do. It was based on God's decision to put everything together for him, which Abraham then entered when he believed.

This same pattern is how we are saved — we believe and then we experience salvation by grace through faith (Ephesians 2:8-9). How did the Lord bring you to the point of belief in Christ for salvation?

4. What have you not seen, because you have not yet believed? Are you taking God at His Word?

Romans 4:13-25

Abraham was fully convinced that God was Who He said He was and that He would perform what He promised. Because Abraham believed, it was credited to him as righteousness (Romans 4:21-22).

1. Deliverance from sin leads to freedom: Read John 8:33-36. Before we come to Christ, we are enslaved to sin. But after we are saved, we are declared righteous and have been sealed by the Holy Spirit, Who sets us free and enables us to obey God and His Word. Are you experiencing freedom in Christ?

2. If you still struggle with sin, does that mean you are not saved?

As we study further in the book of Romans, we will see that even for Christians there is still a struggle between our spirit and flesh (Romans 7:14-25). But once you become a Christian, you have Christ living within you through His Spirit and He enables you to conquer sin. He intercedes for you and empowers you.

3. How are you a child of Abraham according to Romans 4:16-17?

4. Explain verse 17 – "As it is written: *I have made you the father of many nations.* He believed in God, who gives life to the dead and calls things into existence that do not exist."

5. What are you currently believing God for that only He can accomplish?

Hebrews 11:1-6

1. Based upon the verses you just read, write your own definition of faith.

"Faith" — Being persuaded, belief, assent to, and confidence in certain divine truths. (Hebrews 11:1)

2. What is the only way to God?

3. Which person of faith do you admire most in Scripture?

4. What truths can you glean from his or her life?

5. How can you apply these truths to your life?

Isn't Christianity just a myth?

> Simon Greenleaf, the famous Harvard lawyer who wrote a textbook on legal evidence, was converted to Christianity based on his careful examination of the Gospel witnesses from a legal perspective. He concluded that 'copies which had been as universally received and acted upon as the Four Gospels, would have been received in evidence in any court of justice, without the slightest hesitation'.[10]

There are many other people who have studied Christianity to try to disprove it, only to be converted by the overwhelming evidence. Here is a list of a few that you may be interested in and would benefit from reading their books:

Josh McDowell – *More Than a Carpenter, The New Evidence that Demands a Verdict*
Lee Strobel – *The Case for Christ, The Case for a Creator*
Mary Jo Sharp – *Defending the Faith: Apologetics in Women's Ministry, Why Do You Believe That?*

WEEK FOUR

Peace with God

…we have peace with God through our Lord Jesus Christ.
Romans 5:1

Romans 5

In this chapter, Paul expands the implications of justification, God's declaration that the believing sinner is made righteous in Jesus Christ by faith apart from good works. God applied Christ's finished work on the cross to the believer's life, restoring a right standing with God. Those "who believe in Him who raised Jesus our Lord from the dead" (Romans 4:24) can rest assured that their faith has been credited to them as righteousness. This confidence is based on the fact that Christ "was delivered over because of our transgressions, and was raised because of our justification" (Romans 4:25). Without His death, there would be no payment for our sins. Without His resurrection, there would be no proof of the redemptive reality of His death.

⫸ DAY ONE ⫷

Romans 5:1-5

"Therefore, having been justified by faith," (Romans 5:1) we must now learn how to daily live as a follower of Jesus Christ. This slow and often painful process, called sanctification, gradually transforms us to the image of our Lord Jesus. Thankfully "it is God who is at work in [us], both to will and to work for His good pleasure" (Philippians 2:13) throughout this procedure of transformation.

The word "therefore" connects to what Paul had written previously. Therefore, "those who believe in Him" (Romans 4:24) by faith have been declared righteous based on the fact that Jesus died for their sins and was raised again (see Romans 4:25). Justification is God's declaration that the believing sinner is made righteous in Christ by His once-for-all-time sacrifice for sin.

Through a personal relationship with Jesus Christ, "we have peace with God" (Romans 5:1) because the wrath of God has been satisfied by the atoning sacrifice offered by His own Son, Jesus Christ. God's righteousness is judicially imputed (credited to our account) by faith in Him. "He made Him who knew no sin to be sin on our behalf, so that we might become the righteousness of God in Him" (2 Corinthians 5:21). Peace with God is what the gospel produces in the one who has met God on His terms "of repentance toward God and faith in our Lord Jesus Christ" (Acts 20:21). Faith in the Lord Jesus Christ "obtained our introduction by faith into this grace in which we stand" (Romans 5:2) and grants us unhindered access to God the Father.

1. Through Christ we have peace with God. Read Philippians 4:7-9. What benefits do we derive from the peace of God? What things should we dwell on to ensure a mind set on the peace of God? If we practice these things, what promise does God's Word guarantee us?

Because "we have peace with God through our Lord Jesus Christ" (Romans 5:1), "we exult in hope of the glory of God" (Romans 5:2). The believer not only has hope for the future and an eternity in the presence of Christ but also has confidence in the present trials of life. Therefore "we also exult in our tribulations" (Romans 5:3). We do not lose hope during seasons of suffering because we recognize His strong presence in the midst of the crisis. We trust He is building perseverance, proven character, and conviction in us. Furthermore, God is setting His glory on display in and through us as we walk by faith through the season of suffering. When we cannot understand His ways, we can trust His heart "because the love of God has been poured out within our hearts through the Holy Spirit who was given to us" (Romans 5:5). We have received reconciliation through the shed blood of Jesus Christ and now the love of God is experienced in our lives.

2. Read James 1:2-4. This passage parallels today's reading in Romans. What does God produce in us through tribulation?

3. Can you testify to a time God allowed you to walk through a season of suffering? What did He teach you? What Scriptures comforted you?

Why do Christians suffer?

Read the story of the man born blind in John 9:1-3. The disciples asked the Lord who had sinned to cause the man's blindness. What was Jesus' response?

What is one reason Christians suffer?

In Christ, God has declared us justified. In Christ, we have peace with God. In Christ, we have received grace. In Christ, we have hope. In Christ, we have confidence, even in the midst of trials. In Christ, "the love of God has been poured out within our hearts through the Holy Spirit who was given to us" (Romans 5:5). So the question that begs to be answered is, "Are you in Christ?"

Romans 5:6-11

"God demonstrates His own love for us, in that while we were yet sinners Christ died for us" (Romans 5:8). The proof of God's love for us is revealed in that "while we were still helpless, at the right time Christ died for the ungodly" (Romans 5:6). "For if while we were enemies we were reconciled to God through the death of His Son, much more, having been reconciled, we shall be saved by His life" (Romans 5:10). We are saved from the *penalty of sin* by His death (our justification). We are saved from the *power of sin* by His resurrection (our sanctification). And we will one day, when we see Him face to face, be saved from the *presence of sin* by His ascension (our glorification). Therefore, we rejoice, we "also exult in God through our Lord Jesus Christ, through whom we have now received the reconciliation." Romans 5:11

1. Prior to our conversion to Christ we were helpless sinners. Read Ephesians 2:1-3. How does the apostle Paul describe our lost state outside a personal relationship with Christ?

2. Paul adds to his description about our lost condition in Ephesians 2:11-12. What does this passage tell us about our standing apart from Jesus?

We can all agree that it would be a most unusual thing for a person to die in the place of a good man, much less for a wicked one. One of the remarkable things about the death of Christ is that He died for us while we were yet sinners (Romans 5:8). 1 Peter 3:18 says, "For Christ also died for sins once for all, the just for the unjust, so that He might bring us to God, having been put to death in the flesh, but made alive in the spirit." God did not wait until we had earned His love (which, of course, no one could) before He acted in love on our behalf. Christ died for us while we were still enemies.

3. Read I John 3:1-3. What is our reasonable response to the Father's love lavished on us?

God made a way for sinful man to be reconciled to a Holy God by the shed blood of Jesus Christ. He provided forgiveness of sin for all people through the once-for-all death of His Son. 1 John 2:2 says, "He Himself is the propitiation for our sins; and not for ours only, but also for those of the whole world." Reconciliation results in a personal relationship; it cannot be a unilateral action by God alone. Only when that forgiveness is accepted through repentance and faith is the contract completed and salvation secured. God's part is finished; our part is a matter of personal decision.

Our sin debt was paid in Christ. When we received Jesus by grace through faith, cleansing through His blood was applied to our personal sin account, we were forgiven, and God's righteousness was judicially imputed to us. This saves us from the wrath of God, or the eternal punishment of our sin debt in hell. However, the scope of our salvation is *much more* than simply having our sins forgiven and avoiding hell. Since we have been "reconciled to God through the death of His Son . . . we shall be saved by His life" (Romans 5:10). The reference here is to Christ's resurrection, showing that both the death and resurrection are necessary for salvation. By His death we were saved from the penalty of sin. By His resurrection we are saved from the power of sin through His indwelling Holy Spirit. The Spirit of God grants us the power for daily deliverance from the power and dominion of sin. His abiding presence provides the power to rise above the downward pull of the world, the flesh, and the devil. Therefore, "we also exult in God through our Lord Jesus Christ, through whom we have now received the reconciliation." Romans 5:11

4. This passage points to the crucified life, where we are dead to sin and alive to Christ. Read Galatians 2:20. How does Paul describe the Christian life?

5. What must we do in order to live crucified? In what areas of your life are you experiencing the crucified life? In what areas do you need to appropriate the crucified life in order to walk in victory?

How can sinful man be reconciled to a holy God?

Look up the following verses and summarize what they teach us.

Mark 1:14-15

Colossians 1:21-22

Acts 16:22-31

"While we were yet sinners, Christ died for us" (Romans 5:8). We are now reconciled to God through the death of Jesus. "Much more then, having now been justified by His blood, we shall be saved from the wrath of God through Him" (Romans 5:9). We can rest in the knowledge that our salvation is eternally secure and we are safe from the wrath of God in the final judgment. "For if while we were enemies we were reconciled to God through the death of His Son, much more, having been reconciled, we shall be saved by His life" (Romans 5:10). Paul captures the essence of the Christian life in these three verses. We are declared righteous before God at the moment of our salvation (justification). We will be changed into His likeness and will spend eternity in the presence of Christ at the end of our lives (glorification). Until then, we have the life of Christ living in us through the person of the Holy Spirit to empower us to live above the downward pull of the world, the flesh, and the devil. Both the death and resurrection of Christ are necessary for our salvation, which includes our justification, our sanctification, and our glorification.

Romans 5:12-13

Paul writes, "Through one man sin entered into the world, and death through sin, and so death spread to all men, because all sinned" (Romans 5:12). Because Adam was the first created person he represented all who would descend from him. His sin had consequences for all consecutive generations born into the human race.

1. Read Genesis 2:16-17. What was the one prohibition God gave Adam? This was prior to Eve's creation. What can we deduce about God's intention for Adam in regard to his wife?

2. Read Genesis 3:1-6. Who sinned first? After Eve had eaten of the forbidden fruit, what did she do? What did Adam do?

3. Reread Romans 5:12-14. Who did God hold accountable for that sin in the Garden of Eden? Why?

Adam bears the responsibility since he was God's appointed representative of the human race. Adam had a leadership role with respect to all mankind that Eve did not have, even though Eve sinned initially by eating the forbidden fruit. Prior to their sin this couple enjoyed unhindered access to God the Father. They enjoyed His immediate presence "walking in the garden in the cool of the day" (Genesis 3:8). They "were both naked and were not ashamed" (Genesis 2:25). They were guiltless before the Father and uninhibited before each other until Satan and sin marred Paradise. "In the day that you eat from [the tree of the knowledge of good and evil] you will surely die." (Genesis 2:17, brackets mine)

Falling for the beguiling temptation of the serpent, the woman,

> *...took from its fruit and ate; and she gave also to her husband with her, and he ate. Then the eyes of both of them were opened, and they knew that they were naked, and they sewed fig leaves together and made themselves loin coverings. They heard the sound of the LORD God walking in the garden in the cool of the day, and the man and his wife hid themselves from the presence of the LORD God among the trees of the garden. Then the LORD God called to the man, and said to him, "Where are you?" He said, "I heard the sound of You in the garden, and I was afraid because I was naked; so I hid myself.* (Genesis 3:6-10)

The serpent had lied promising they would be "like God, knowing good and evil" (Genesis. 3:5). Instead, new emotions of shame, guilt, and fear were immediately experienced by the couple.

4. Read Genesis 3:11-13. When God confronted Adam with his sin, how did Adam respond? What was Eve's response?

Sadly, neither Adam nor Eve would accept their part in their sin. Adam and Eve experienced spiritual death and separation from God. Adam and Eve died immediately in their spirits, progressively in their souls, and ultimately in their bodies. "Through one man sin entered into the world, and death through sin, and so death spread to all men" (Romans 5:12). Because Adam was the firstborn of mankind, he was the federal head of the human race, and thus his sin had ramifications on all future generations.

The bad news is that Adam brought sin and death into the world. The good news of the gospel is that Christ has reversed the consequences of Adam's sin by His death, burial, and resurrection. Hallelujah! What a Savior!

Romans 5:14-17

We are identified with Adam as the head of the human race. His sin became our sin; his death became our death. Adam pictures the sinful condition and lost state of all humans. Jesus stands for the justification received by grace through faith.

1. Read 1 Corinthians 15:47. What insight do you gain from this verse?

In creation Adam was a picture, "a type of Him who was to come" (Romans 5:14). Adam is an Old Testament image of Christ as the covenantal head of all humankind. God said, "'Let Us make man in Our image, according to Our likeness; and let them rule over the fish of the sea and over the birds of the sky and over the cattle and over all the earth, and over every creeping thing that creeps on the earth.' God created man in His image, in the image of God He created him; male and female He created them" (Genesis 1:26-27). Adam and Eve were created in the image of God and given authority to rule over God's entire creation. Then sin entered the picture. Adam, *the first man*, sinned and gave away the estate of mankind to Satan. Adam's sin caused all future generations to be born in his likeness, bearing the birthmark of his sin nature. Jesus, *the Second Man*, made a way for sinful man to be recreated or born again for all who will turn to Him in faith.

Everyone is either in Adam (having been born once) and or in Christ (having been born again). Paul wrote, "In Adam all die, so also in Christ all will be made alive"(1 Corinthians 15:22). The disobedience of the first Adam brought sin, sorrow, and suffering upon the human race resulting in death, condemnation, and eternal punishment in hell. The Last Adam, Jesus Christ, brought righteousness, justification, and eternal life resulting in salvation to all who believe by faith.

"The gift is not like that which came through the one who sinned" (Romans 5:16). God's act of grace was out of proportion to the offense of Adam. Adam's sin led to the condemnation and death of the entire human race. God's grace is infinitely greater for good than Adam's sin is for evil. The gift of God's grace leading to salvation transforms for eternity the life and destiny of all who are in Christ.

2. Look up Romans 6:23. What are the wages of sin (the just reward for man's sin) beginning with Adam? What has been gifted to us in Christ Jesus?

Sin, resulting in separation from God and death, entered the world through Adam. In light of that reality, how much more will those receiving the abundant grace of God and His gift of righteousness reign in life (now and throughout eternity) through the one man Jesus Christ! The sin of one man (Adam) caused death to reign. The obedience of One Man (Jesus) brings triumph over death to all who believe. Sin is the ruin; Christ is the remedy!

Read Romans 5:18-21

Adam's sin plunged the human race into condemnation. Jesus paid the penalty of sin once for all but His blood is only applied to those who receive Him with repentance and faith.

1. Read John 3:16-21. To whom did God give *His only begotten Son?* How does one gain eternal life? How does this passage describe those who refuse to come to Jesus for salvation? How does this passage describe those who believe in Him?

God gave the Law to reveal His holy standard and prove our inability to keep it. Romans 3:20 says, "By the works of the Law no flesh will be justified in His sight; for through the Law comes the knowledge of sin." The Law was never intended to provide salvation but to convince people of their need for a Savior. Christ fulfilled the Law and supplied what the Law could not supply--salvation from sin.

2. Read Galatians 3:21-29. What was the purpose of the law?

The reign of sin brought death and eternal separation from God, but grace abounded all the more (Romans 5:20). Sin no longer reigns, grace does. "For of His fullness we have all received, and grace upon grace. For the Law was given through Moses; grace and truth were realized through Jesus Christ" (John 1:16-17). Eternity in hell is the fate of those who reject Christ--a self-inflicted penalty for rejecting Jesus rather than accepting His gracious gift of salvation. Those who receive the imputed righteousness of Christ Jesus will reap life eternal. Jesus said, "These will go away into eternal punishment, but the righteous into eternal life." Matthew 25:46

3. Reread Romans 5:1-21. Make a comparison of the results of being in Adam as opposed to be in Christ.

In Adam	In Christ

When Adam (mankind's representative) sinned, God declared the whole human race guilty. Adam's sin precipitated the downfall of the human race. God made a way for guilty sinners to be reconciled to a holy God through Jesus Christ. We must individually repent, believe, and receive Jesus by faith. An unbeliever who "was dead in transgressions, [was] made alive together with Christ, having been saved through faith" (see Ephesians 2:1-8). "God rescued us from the domain of darkness and transferred us to the kingdom of His beloved Son, in whom we have redemption, the forgiveness of sins" (Colossians 1:13-14). In that divine transaction, Christ's righteousness was imputed to us. God "made Him who knew no sin to be sin on our behalf, so that we might become the righteousness of God in Him." 2 Corinthians 5:21

WEEK FIVE

A Work in Progress

*Knowing this, that our old self was crucified with Him, in order that our body of
sin might be done away with, so that we would no longer be slaves to sin;
for he who has died is freed from sin.*

Romans 6:6

Romans 6-7

In these two chapters Paul turns his attention to the process of sanctification, the lifelong process of transformation into the likeness of Christ. Our salvation ensures our sin debt has been paid in full. We are free from the penalty of sin which is separation from God and eternity in hell. However, daily we still struggle with the flesh, "the law of sin which is in my members" (Romans 7:23). Recurring sinful habit patterns of our lives prior to a personal relationship with Christ continue to wage war against us. In these two chapters Paul reveals how we can have victory over the old nature.

⫸ DAY ONE ⫷

Romans 6:1-14

Romans 6 deals with believers' relationship to sin because we are identified with Christ in His death, burial, and resurrection. In Christ, we are the happy recipients of the grace of God. Living under grace can be distorted. Paul addresses this misconception. Romans 6:1 says, "What shall we say then? Are we to continue in sin so that grace may increase? May it never be!"

We have all experienced the ditch on either side of grace. On one side is *legalism,* while on the other is *license*. Legalism reduces the Christian walk to strictly adhering to a list of rules and regulations.

1. Read Colossians 2:20-23. Paul is addressing the issue of legalism that was prevalent in the early church and continues to haunt us. How does Paul identify legalism?

Legalism gives "the appearance of wisdom in self-made religion and self-abasement and severe treatment of the body, but [is] of no value against fleshly indulgences" (Colossians 2:23). Legalism is an attempt to control the flesh externally by strict adherence to rules and regulations. Such severe treatment of the body does not result in a long-term solution to the internal problem of the flesh.

The other side of the ditch is *license*. License casually dismisses sin while claiming the covering of grace. The gift of God through the Lord Jesus Christ is a free gift, but salvation carries with it a call to personal holiness and practical righteousness. Christ died for us. Surely we can live for Him!

2. Read 1 Thessalonians 2:11-12. As children of God we have received God's grace. What should be the natural response to the One who has poured out His grace on us?

Through our salvation we have "been baptized into Christ Jesus"(Romans 6:3) by the operation of the Holy Spirit of God. When Christ died, we died. When Christ was raised, we were "raised from the dead through the glory of the Father, so we too might walk in newness of life" (Romans 6:4). Christ broke the power of sin and put it out of commission through our identification with Jesus. The "old self was crucified with Him, in order that our body of sin might be done away with, so that we would no longer be slaves to sin" (Romans 6:6). Paul is not suggesting we can achieve sinless perfection, rather he reminds us we are no longer held captive by sin. "For we also once were foolish ourselves, disobedient, deceived, enslaved to various lusts and pleasures, spending our life in malice and envy, hateful, hating one another. But when the kindness of God our Savior and His love for mankind appeared, He saved us." Titus 3:3-5

Paul is not diminishing the threat that sin poses to Christian living. Sin remains a temptation that must be battled daily. Paul maintains that believers have been put into a decisively new relationship to sin, a relationship in which "we would no longer be slaves to sin; for he who has died is freed from sin" (Romans 6:6-7). Sin no longer has the power to master us or hold us in bondage, apart from our decision to allow it to run unchecked in our lives.

"Now if we have died with Christ, we believe that we shall also live with Him" (Romans 6:8). This is not a promise regarding life in heaven after death. This is a promise of the abundant life in Christ (see John 10:10) available now in this life. The Christian life is not (or should not be) a passive existence but rather the aggressive pursuit of spiritual maturity. The standard pattern for the Christian life should result in progressive spiritual growth with us "being transformed . . . from glory to glory." 2 Corinthians 3:18

The victorious Christian life is *available* to all believers, but it is *not automatic*. "Even so consider yourselves to be dead to sin but alive to God in Christ Jesus. Therefore do not let sin reign in your mortal body so that you obey its lusts" (Romans 6:11-12). We must aggressively pursue a life of personal holiness and practical righteousness. Paul wrote, "Be diligent to present yourself approved to God as a workman who does not need to be ashamed, accurately handling the word of truth" (2 Timothy 2:15). The forward progress of the sanctification process is greatly advanced when we apply ourselves to the spiritual disciplines such as personal Bible study, prayer, memorization of Scriptures, and regular involvement with a Bible-believing church, just to name a few.

3. Many believers have been lulled into believing God alone works the process of sanctification without our involvement. Nothing could be further from the truth! Read 2 Peter 1:5-9. What is required of us? What are the results of spiritual diligence? If we fail to pursue personal godliness what is the result? What does the lack of these qualities in the life of a believer indicate?

We must "consider [ourselves] to be dead to sin, but alive to God in Christ Jesus" (Romans 6:11). Our identification with Christ must be appropriated (believed and acted upon) in order to activate the power of Christ in our lives. The mastery of sin has been broken through Christ. We must reckon it to be true in our individual lives. Reckoning is a step of faith that believes God's Word and acts upon it, in spite of circumstances or feelings.

"Therefore do not let sin reign in your mortal body so that you obey its lusts" (Romans 6:12). God has broken the power of sin but we are required to walk in obedience to the Word of God, dependence on the Spirit of God, and confidence in the Son of God. "For it is God who is at work in you, both to will and to work for His good pleasure" (Philippians 2:13). By faith we obey and step into the abundant life God has accomplished for us.

Prior to conversion, we presented "the members of [our] body to sin as instruments of unrighteousness" (Romans 6:13). We were the trapped by "the snare of the devil, having been held captive by him to do his will" (2 Timothy 2:26). Now in Christ we are free to "present [ourselves] to God as those alive from the dead, and [our] members as instruments of righteousness to God" (Romans 6:13). In John 8:36 Jesus said, 'So if the Son makes you free, you will be free indeed." As believers we are free to choose. Either we choose to yield the members of our body to Satan for sin or we choose to crucify our flesh and experience victory in our Christian lives.

Romans 6:15-23

Paul asks a second rhetorical question, "Shall we sin because we are not under law but under grace? May it never be!" (Romans 6:15). Grace does not free us to abandon God's demand for righteous living. Grace sets us free from the bondage of sin and grants us the ability to live to the glory of God.

Paul sets forth two masters: one is sin and the other is Christ. Prior to our conversion, we were slaves to sin, self, and Satan. Consequently, we functioned only subject "to the wages of sin [which] is death" (Romans 6:23). Through our conversion, we exchanged one master for another. Servitude to sin was replaced with servitude to God. God grants His servants eternal life and freedom from sin's destructive power. "Do you not know that when you present yourselves to someone as slaves for obedience, you are slaves of the one whom you obey, either of sin resulting in death, or of obedience resulting in righteousness?" (Romans 6:16). To choose sin results in death. To choose obedience to Christ, results in righteousness. There is no middle ground and there must not be any compromise. We have been "freed from sin" and have become "slaves of righteousness" (Romans 6:18). This divine transaction should become progressively evident in our lives.

1. Read Ephesians 4:22-32. Paul urges us to lay aside the old manner of life when we were slaves to sin and put on the new self, which in the likeness of God has been created in righteousness and holiness of truth. Make a list of the characteristics noted in this passage of our lives prior to and after our conversion.

The Old Manner of Life	The New Self in Christ

To begin to unravel Romans 6, we need a working understanding of these three words: know, reckon, and yield. We must *know* "that our old self was crucified with Him . . . so that we would no longer be slaves to sin; for he who has died is freed from sin" (Romans 6:6-7). We must *reckon* or "consider [ourselves] to be dead to sin, but alive to God in Christ Jesus" (Romans 6:11). And we must *yield* our "members as instruments of righteousness to God" (Romans 6:13). To advance in sanctification, we should regularly spend time with the Lord in His Word. Through personal Bible study, we will *know* our position in Christ. We will have the faith to *reckon* ourselves dead to sin and alive to God. And we will be able to *yield* ourselves to the indwelling Holy Spirit and walk in His ways. Acting on these truths leads to daily victory over the flesh. "But now having been freed from sin and enslaved to God, you derive your benefit, resulting in sanctification, and the outcome, eternal life." Romans 6:22

Romans 7:1-6

Romans 6 dealt with the believer's new relationship with sin through identification with Christ. Romans 7 addresses the believer's relationship to the Law. Paul uses the marriage relationship to illustrate our relationship to the Law as New Testament believers. A wife is bound to her husband until death separates them. "If her husband dies, she is released from the law concerning her husband" (Romans 7:2). His death releases her to be joined to another. Prior to our conversion, we were bound by the Law. The Law could not provide victory over sin and death, but those who have been saved have died with Christ and are set free from sin and the Law. We are no longer "married" to a sacrificial system of regulations. We are now "married" to Jesus Christ and the Law has no control over us.

As New Testament believers we do not discount or disregard the Law. In Matthew 5:17 Jesus said, "Do not think that I came to abolish the Law or the Prophets; I did not come to abolish but to fulfill." Now under grace our obligations of obedience are even greater than they were under the Law. Jesus taught in the Sermon on the Mount (see Matthew 5:1-7:29) to go beyond outward actions and deal with inward attitudes. We do not merely adhere to a set of rules; we obey the Spirit of God who fulfills the righteousness of the Law in us from a heart of love and devotion. "Therefore, my brethren, you also were made to die to the Law through the body of Christ, so that you might be joined to another, to Him who was raised from the dead, in order that we might bear fruit for God." Romans 7:4

1. Read John 15:1-8. Jesus is the true Vine. What is the relationship between the branch and the Vine? What is the result of abiding in the Vine? How is the Father glorified? What is the proof of our relationship with the Lord?

Paul prayed we would "be sincere and blameless until the day of Christ; having been filled with the fruit of righteousness, which comes through Jesus Christ, to the glory and praise of God" (Philippians 1:10-11). We are set apart and identified as Christ-followers by our good works produced by obedience to the Word of God and dependence on the Spirit of God.

2. Read Galatians 5:22-23. Make a list of attributes of the fruit of the Spirit. The word "fruit" is singular because these descriptive characteristics are evidence of the Lord's work in the lives of yielded believers.

Titus 3:5 says, "He saved us, not on the basis of deeds which we have done in righteousness, but according to His mercy, by the washing of regeneration and renewing by the Holy Spirit." We are not saved by good works, but good works give evidence to a genuine conversion experience. "For we are His workmanship, created in Christ Jesus for good works, which God prepared beforehand so that we would walk in them." Ephesians 2:10

No longer are we in bondage to vain attempts to keep the Law but now we are freed to operate in the Spirit. "Now we have been released from the Law, having died to that by which we were bound, so that we serve in newness of the Spirit and not in oldness of the letter." Romans 7:6

Romans 7:7-13

All mankind is sinful and rebellious against God. Romans 3:10 says, "There is none righteous; not even one." Romans 3:23 has a similar message, "For all have sinned and fall short of the glory of God." Paul reasons that sin cannot be exposed or measured apart from its rejection of a specific commandment of God. Through the Law of God, Paul came to see himself as a sinner. In Romans 7:7 Paul wrote, "I would not have come to know sin except through the Law; for I would not have known about coveting if the Law had not said, 'You shall not covet.'" The prohibition against coveting stimulated the desire to sin, and sin led to spiritual death. "Sin became alive and I died," stated Paul. Romans 7:9

1. Read Galatians 3:24-26. What was the purpose of the Law?

The Law was given to reveal God's holiness and our sinfulness. The Law was given to make us realize we are unable to meet God's holy standard of perfect righteousness. The Law was given to reveal our need for a Savior.

The Law reveals our sin but cannot redeem us. "By the works of the Law no flesh will be justified in His sight, for through the Law comes the knowledge of sin" (Romans 3:20). Having been confronted with our sinful nature revealed through the Law, we are forced to make a decision about Jesus, the only One who can deal with our sin.

2. Read the story of Nicodemus in John 3:1-15. What must one do to be saved? What Old Testament leader did Jesus cite? What truth from that imagery was He relating to his discussion with Nicodemus?

"The Law is holy, and the commandment is holy and righteous and good" (Romans 7:12). The Law reveals the horrendous true nature of our sin which is "utterly sinful" (Romans 7:13) in the light of the divine perfection required by the Law.

Romans 7:14-25

In this section, Paul addresses the internal conflict common to all believers. Understanding the relationship between believers and indwelling sin is paramount to the matter of sanctification. Believers want to please God, but find themselves frustrated in their efforts due to the lingering presence of sin which dwells in us. In Romans 7:15 he wrote, "For what I am doing, I do not understand; for I am not practicing what I would like to do, but I am doing the very thing I hate." Although we have been redeemed, the flesh remains. In simplest terms, the flesh is the residual habit patterns left over from our unregenerate state prior to our conversion. The flesh continually attempts to influence our mind, will, and emotions to gain control of our behavior. "The good that I want, I do not do, but I practice the very evil that I do not want. But if I am doing the very thing I do not want, I am no longer the one doing it, but sin which dwells in me" (Romans 7:19-20). Paul acknowledges the indwelling principle of sin that once owned him as a slave and continues to express itself through his mind and body.

1. Read Galatians 5:16-17. How can we avoid carrying out the desires of the flesh? Describe our internal struggle.

In Romans 7:22-23 Paul writes, "I joyfully concur with the law of God in the inner man, but I see a different law in the members of my body, waging war against the law of my mind and making me a prisoner of the law of sin which is in my members." Indwelling sin continues to wage "war against the law of our mind" in an attempt to make us prisoners "of the law of sin" in the same way it operated prior to our conversion. As Christians, we will still struggle with sin until the time of our departure through death or the rapture of the church.

2. Read 1 John 1:9. Thankfully God has made a way for us to deal with our sins after our conversion. What must we do? What has God promised?

A believer's identification with Jesus Christ's death and resurrection does not make him/her immune from the downward pull of the indwelling sin nature. In Romans 7:24 Paul expresses his frustration, "Wretched man that I am! Who will set me free from the body of this death?" Paul recognized the lifelong internal conflict warring in his mortal body.

Paul answered his own question. "Thanks be to God through Jesus Christ our Lord!" One day we will be fully redeemed and delivered from the presence of sin. "For our citizenship is in heaven, from which also we eagerly wait for a Savior, the Lord Jesus Christ; who will transform the body of our humble state into conformity with the body of His glory" (Philippians 3:20-21).

Until that day we must engage in spiritual warfare.

3.   Read 2 Corinthians 10:3-5. Describe the weapons of our warfare. What do these weapons allow us to do?

Paul said, "So then, on the one hand I myself with my mind am serving the law of God, but on the other, with my flesh the law of sin" (Romans 7:25). As long as we occupy these mortal bodies, *the law of sin* will be present in us. But God has given us the Word of God as our external control and the Spirit of God as our internal control. By faith we can tear down strongholds of habitual sinful patterns, and take "every thought captive to the obedience of Christ" (2 Corinthians 10:5). Christ has gained the victory for us in this life and the next, but we must fight the good fight of faith.

Why is Jesus' resurrection so central to Christianity?

With so much emphasis on the cross of Jesus, one might wonder why the resurrection of Jesus is of such paramount importance.

The resurrection witnesses to the immense power of God Himself. Only God who created life can resurrect it after death. Only He can remove the sting and gain the victory over the grave. Read 1 Corinthians 15:54-55 and write down your insights.

Christ's resurrection authenticated His own claims that He would be raised on the third day. Read Mark 8:31; 9:31; and 10:34 and record your thoughts.

The resurrection validated the Old Testament prophecies. Read Acts 17:2-3 and write out your thoughts.

The resurrection empathically declared Christ to be the Son of God. Read Romans 1:1-4 and write out your insights.

If Jesus is not resurrected, we have no hope that we will be. Apart from Christ's resurrection we have no Savior, no salvation, and no hope of eternal life. Look up 1 Corinthians 15:14-19 and make notes on your insights.

Jesus is the first fruits of all who die in Christ. Read 1 Corinthians 15:20-21 and write down your thoughts.

Jesus Christ died, was buried, and rose on the third day according to the Scriptures (see 1 Corinthians 15:3-4). And He is coming again! "The Lord Himself will descend from heaven with a shout, with the voice of the archangel and with the trumpet of God, and the dead in Christ will rise first. Then we who are alive and remain will be caught up together with them in the clouds to meet the Lord in the air, and so we shall always be with the Lord. Therefore comfort one another with these words" (1 Thessalonians 4:16-18). Why is Jesus' resurrection so central to Christianity? The resurrection of Jesus proves Jesus is the Son of God and that God accepted His sacrifice on our behalf. The resurrection shows God has the power to raise us from the dead. It guarantees that those who die in Christ will not remain, but will be resurrected unto eternal life.

WEEK SIX

Free Indeed

Therefore there is now no condemnation for those who are in Christ Jesus.
For the law of the Spirit of life in Christ Jesus has set you free from the law of sin and of death.
Romans 8:1-2

Romans 8

In this chapter, Paul continues writing about our sanctification, the phase between our justification and glorification whereby we are progressively conformed to the image of Jesus Christ. In this chapter, the role of the Holy Spirit is presented as central to this process. In John 8:36 Jesus said, "So if the Son makes you free, you will be free indeed."

 DAY ONE

Romans 8:1-4

In Romans 7, Paul commiserates with us over the dilemma of the indwelling sin which remains in the believer after conversion. In Romans 7:24 he laments, "Wretched man that I am! Who will set me free from the body of this death?" In Romans 7:25 he rejoices in his conclusion, "Thanks be to God through Jesus Christ our Lord!" Jesus has set us free from the law of sin and death.

Paul writes, "Therefore (referring to Romans 7:25) there is now no condemnation for those who are in Christ Jesus" (Romans 8:1, parenthesis mine). That's good news! Prior to our conversion, we were under God's judgment. Now in Christ, we are standing in His imputed righteousness under God's grace. Good news indeed!

One might argue, "How is that possible since we continue to sin even after conversion?" Paul clearly states there is no condemnation because "the law of the Spirit of life in Christ Jesus has set [us] free from the law of sin and death" (Romans 8:2). Christ's finished work on the cross provides the basis for the deliverance of believers from God's judgment. The gift of the indwelling Holy Spirit provides the power to overcome the daily temptations of sin brought about by the indwelling principle of sin.

1. James records the evolution of sin, tracking it from the seed thought of temptation to full-blown behavior. Read James 1:13-15. What are the progressive stages of sin? What set these steps into motion? What steps can you take to stop the sinful thought before it becomes a sinful action?

The Law revealed God's righteous standard and identified sin, but was powerless to conquer sin in us due to the exceedingly sinful nature of our fallen nature. "For what the Law could not do, weak as it was through the flesh, God did: sending His own Son in the likeness of sinful flesh and as an offering for sin, He condemned sin in the flesh." Romans 8:3

During His incarnation, Jesus became a man without diminishing His deity and retained His deity without diminishing His humanity. Fully man. Fully God. Hebrews 2:17 says, "Therefore, He had to be made like His brethren in all things, so that He might become a merciful and faithful high priest in things pertaining to God, to make propitiation for the sins of the people." He was the God Man who became a merciful and faithful high priest in order to become the once-for-all time atoning sacrifice for the sins of the people.

2. Read Hebrews 2:14-15. Christ identified with us that we might identify with Him by grace through faith. What are some of the benefits we reap from His sacrifice in regard to death?

The fear of death has held mankind captive since the beginning of time. By the death and resurrection of Jesus, sin's debt was paid in full and He rendered Satan powerless, freeing us from the power of death and its sway to produce fear.

The death of Christ provides forgiveness of sin and imputes God's righteousness to all who believe by faith in Him. The life of Christ through the indwelling Holy Spirit of God empowers us to walk in obedience. "The requirement of the Law [is] fulfilled in us, who do not walk according to the flesh but according to the Spirit." Romans 8:4

Romans 8:5-8

In this passage, Paul continues to point to the indwelling Holy Spirit as the origin of "life and peace" (Romans 8:6) in the believer. He contrasts the carnal Christian with the victorious believer. The casual or carnal believer has set his/her mind on "the things of the flesh" as opposed to "the things of the Spirit." Romans 8:5

Carnal Christians set their minds on the things of the flesh. "The mind set on the flesh is death" (Romans 8:6). Here Paul is speaking of spiritual death. To "set the mind on the flesh" is to continually desire the things in this world rather than those of the Lord. John wrote, "Do not love the world nor the things of the world" (1 John 2:15). James, the brother of Jesus, elaborated, "You adulteresses, do you now know that friendship with the world is hostility toward God? Therefore whoever wishes to be a friend of the world makes himself an enemy of God" (James 4:4). Carnality in the believer results in a damaged testimony for Christ in this life and the loss of eternal rewards in the next.

1. Look at Galatians 6:8-9. This passage explains the natural consequences of sowing to the flesh. What are they? What does the one who sows to the Spirit reap?

2. In addition, this passage (Galatians 6:8-9) carries a warning and a promise in it. What are they? Jot down some ideas for avoiding growing weary in the Christian life.

Carnality is a blight on the body of Christ. The carnal believer has a saved soul but a wasted life! The resulting lifestyle is one that closely parallels the life prior to conversion. The carnal believer does not lose his/her salvation, but certainly damages his/her witness, invalidates the power of Christ to change a life, and will suffer the loss of eternal reward.

3. Read 1 Corinthians 3:11-15. In this passage, Paul is speaking to believers, those who have laid the foundation of Christ. At the Bema Judgment (2 Corinthians 5:10) the believer is judged, not for his/her sins (Jesus took that on the cross), but in regard to his/her service (works of righteousness built on the foundation of Christ) for the Kingdom of God. Paul is contrasting the difference between the rewards of a life well-lived for Christ with those of the carnal believer. What rewards will be given to the victorious Christian? What will the carnal believer receive?

As we saw in I Corinthians 3:15, the carnal Christian is saved and will go to heaven, "yet so as through fire." Carnal Christians have "set their minds on the things of the flesh" (Romans 8:5). Paul writes, "The mind set on the flesh is hostile towards God; for it does not subject itself to the law of God, for it is not even able to do so, and those who are in the flesh cannot please God" (Romans 8:7). Those who operate in the flesh rather than in the Spirit behave as the unredeemed and cannot please God.

In similar fashion, the unbeliever who is totally "in the flesh" without the indwelling Holy Spirit "cannot please God" (Romans 8:8). Many commentators believe Paul is inserting a reference to unbelievers at this point as opposed to speaking of carnal Christians. The unsaved lead lives totally void of spiritual life. Paul notes in 1 Corinthians 2:14, "A natural man does not accept the things of the Spirit of God, for they are foolishness to him; and he cannot understand them, because they are spiritually appraised." It appears Paul is reminding us that the carnal Christian's behavior mirrors the lifestyle of those who live outside a personal relationship with Christ.

God intends a much more fulfilling life for us in Christ than the casual Christian discovers, primarily because of the lack of spiritual growth. Stunted spiritual growth, for whatever reason, results in a believer who does not reach his/her potential in Christ.

Romans 8:9-14

In our passage today, Paul reiterates that the difference between those outside a personal relationship with Christ and genuine followers of Christ is the indwelling Spirit of God. "However, you are not in the flesh but in the Spirit, if indeed the Spirit of God dwells in you. But if anyone does not have the Spirit of Christ, he does not belong to Him" (Romans 8:9). The Spirit of God gives spiritual life and apart from Him one cannot be related to Christ.

1. Read Ephesians 1:13-14. What happened when we were born again? How does Paul describe the Holy Spirit in regard to the believer?

The Spirit of God is God's guarantee of our future glorification when we see Jesus through the portal of death or the Rapture of the church. The indwelling Spirit gives us confidence to believe in the eternal security of the believer.

2. John wrote extensively on eternal life. Look up passages below. What do we learn about the gift of eternal life?

    John 3:15-16

    John 17:3

    1 John 5:11-13

In John 14:1-3 Jesus said, "Do not let your heart be troubled; believe in God, believe also in Me. In My Father's house are many dwelling places; if it were not so, I would have told you; for I go to prepare a place for you. If I go and prepare a place for you, I will come again and receive you to Myself, that where I am there you may be also." One day we will be in the presence of the Lord forever. Until then, we overcome the power of sin by the power of the indwelling Holy Spirit.

In Romans 8:11 Paul writes, "If the Spirit of Him who raised Jesus from the dead dwells in [us], He who raised Christ Jesus from the dead will also give life to [our] mortal bodies through His Spirit who dwells in [us]." As believers we are under obligation not to "live according to the flesh"(Romans 8:12), but through the Spirit of the Lord. "For all who are being led by the Spirit of God . . . are sons and daughters of God" (Romans 8:14). As such, we are to refuse to give in to the temptations of the lusts of the flesh; rather, we are to enjoy the fullness of our lives in Christ.

Romans 8:15-25

Through a personal relationship with Christ, we have "not received a spirit of slavery leading to fear again, but [we] have received a spirit of adoption as sons by which we cry out, 'Abba! Father!'" (Romans 8:15). God the Father has adopted us into His family. Through Christ we can approach God as a child does his/her daddy. In Bible times, adopted sons enjoyed the same privileges as natural-born sons. Instead of fear, we have faith in our standing before the Father. Furthermore, we have become His children through the new birth. "The Spirit Himself testifies with our spirit that we are children of God, and if children, heirs also, heirs of God and fellow heirs with Christ" (Romans 8:16). John 1:12 says, "But as many as received Him, to them He gave the right to become children of God, even to those who believe in His name." We share equally in all the riches of God's kingdom now and in the future with the Lord Jesus.

Sharing with the Lord in riches of the kingdom of God involves sharing in His suffering as well. To be sure, sin causes suffering, even as Christ suffered for our sin (see 1 Peter 3:18). But not all suffering is the result of sin. 2 Timothy 3:12 says, "Indeed, all who desire to live godly in Christ Jesus will be persecuted."

1. Look up 1 Peter 4:12-14. How should we view suffering for the cause of Christ?

Despite the threat of suffering and even impending martyrdom Paul declared, "For I consider that the sufferings of this present time are not worthy to be compared with the glory that is to be revealed to us" (Romans 8:18). The future glory is so great that any present sufferings are insignificant by comparison. It would appear that intrinsic in his words is Paul's desire for us to adopt the same attitude.

2. Read 2 Corinthians 4:17-18. How does Paul describe the sufferings of this life? What does it produce in us? How can we maintain an eternal viewpoint during our time on planet earth?

Suffering serves to break our attachment to this life and cause us to long for the next.

When Adam sinned, "the creation was subjected to futility" (Romans 8:20). In judgment God said to Adam, "Cursed is the ground because of you" (Genesis 3:17). All of creation "groans and suffers the pains of childbirth together until now "(Romans 8:22). At the end of the age 'there will no longer be any curse" (Revelation 22:3). The Lord will deliver the entire creation from bondage and all nature will return to its original created glory.

Not only does God's creation long to "be set free from its slavery to corruption "(Romans 8:21) and the effects of sin, "we ourselves groan within ourselves, waiting eagerly for our adoption as sons, the redemption of our body" (Romans 8:23). We are currently enjoying many of the privileges of adoption, but they will pale in comparison to the glory of our resurrection. All of this serves to remind us that we are "aliens and strangers"(1 Peter 2:11) and this is not our home! Therefore, "we hope for what we do not see, with perseverance we wait eagerly for it" (Romans 8:25) as we are "looking for the blessed hope and the appearing of the glory of our great God and Savior, Jesus Christ" (Titus 2:13). Hallelujah! What a Savior!

Romans 8:26-39

All of creation groans, longing to be released from the curse of this life and be swept into the presence of the Lord forever. But how shall we live until that time? Surely our faith in Christ provides something more substantial for the present than to simply wait for our glorious future in heaven. Paul brings us back to the role the Spirit of God plays in our Christian life prior to our glorification. He writes "In the same way the Spirit also helps our weakness; for we do not know how to pray as we should, but the Spirit Himself intercedes for us with groanings too deep for words" (Romans 8:26). Thank you, Jesus. As if to strengthen our weary souls, Paul reminds us of the indwelling Holy Spirit and the privilege of prayer.

1. Read Philippians 4:6-9. What is God's cure for anxiety? What is the result of a praying life? How can we maintain the peace of God even in the midst of troubling circumstances?

Through prayer, an anxious child connects to the heart of his/her Father and the peace of God and the presence of God attends to his/her troubled soul.

Furthermore, we can rest in the knowledge that God is causing "all things to work together for good to those who love God, to those who are called according to His purpose. For those whom He foreknew, He also predestined to become conformed to the image of His Son, so that He would be the firstborn among many brethren; and these whom He predestined, He also called; and these whom He called, He also justified; and these whom He justified, He also glorified" (Romans 8:28-30). While we cannot fully unravel the theology in Paul's words, we can trust God and rest in His sovereign purposes and plans. He is bringing about our conformity to Christ, strengthening our fellowship with Him, producing fruits of righteousness in lives, and preparing us to spend eternity in His presence.

Paul does not comfort his readers by denying the difficulties believers will experience in this life. Rather he builds the argument of our secure position in Christ. As he exclaims in Romans 8:31, "If God is for us, who can be against us?"

2. What does 1 John 4:4 say?

We are overcomers! We may be required to endure hardships but the world, the flesh, and/or Satan will not succeed. We can rest in the knowledge that God will prevail.

God "did not spare His own Son, but delivered Him over for us all, how will He not also with Him freely give us all things" (Romans 8:32). God has already given us His greatest gift in Christ. Surely we can trust Him even when circumstances seem threatening.

Paul reminds us of the intercessory ministry of the Lord "who was raised, who is at the right hand of God, [and] who also intercedes for us" (Romans 8:34). Jesus is seated at the right hand of the Father and He is praying for us!

In Romans 8:35 Paul asks, "Who will separate us from the love of Christ? Will tribulation, or distress, or persecution, or famine, or nakedness, or peril, or sword?" The inference is that no one and nothing can separate us from the Lord Jesus Christ.

3. Read John 10:27-30. In this passage believers are pictured as sheep. What does John tell us about our Good Shepherd? Is it possible for any one to snatch His sheep out of His hand? Why not?

We can trust the Lord even in the midst of difficult circumstances. We are winning an overwhelming victory through the One who had loved us enough to die for us! We are not victims of life's difficulties. We are victors who have experienced the presence of the Lord in the midst of suffering and who trust the peace of the Lord to sustain us.

God is at work in all the circumstances of life to conform us to the image of His Son. Such is the process of sanctification. Hard times will come, but nothing "will be able to separate us from the love of God, which is in Christ Jesus our Lord" (Romans 8:39). Romans 8 begins with the glorious truth of no condemnation in Christ and ends with the equally glorious truth of no separation from Christ.

Is God all-powerful?

The Bible speaks of God as all-powerful or omnipotent. Here is a selection of verses to validate God's omnipotence.

Genesis 1:1

Psalm 33:9

Genesis 17:1

Jeremiah 32:27

Matthew 19:26

Colossians 1:17

Hebrews 1:3

God is able to do anything that is consistent with His holy character. "Hallelujah! For the Lord our God, the Almighty, reigns" (Revelation 19:6). Hallelujah! What a Savior!

WEEK SEVEN
Same Lord Over All

For there is no distinction between Jew and Greek; for the same
Lord is Lord of all, abounding in riches for all who call on Him.
Romans 10:12

As we concluded last week's study on Romans 8, we were encouraged by the powerful promise found in verses 38-39 where Paul related that nothing can separate us from the love of God. Then suddenly in chapters 9-11, Paul's letter to the Romans took a different turn—some have called it a parenthesis and others a digression. In truth, Paul's message was foundational in explaining the nature of Almighty God and His redemptive relationship to both the Jews and the Gentiles. The saga of Israel's adoption as God's chosen people was chronicled through the Old Testament with God's call of Abraham, His deliverance from Egypt, the settlement in Canaan, the Israelites' disobedience and idolatry, their captivity and the eventual return of a remnant to the land. Next on God's timetable was the arrival of Jesus the Messiah. And so God fulfilled His plan to provide salvation for mankind through the line of Abraham. Yet for the most part, Israel rejected God's provision.

He came to His own, and those who were His own did not receive Him. But as many as received Him, to
them He gave the right to become children of God, even to those who believe in His name. John 1:11-12

>>> DAY ONE <<<

Romans 9:1-18

As Paul reflected on Israel's rejection of Jesus and God's mercy in extending salvation to the Gentiles, he showed a heart of tenderness for his brethren that should challenge us.

1. What brought great sorrow to Paul? What was he willing to do as a result?

2. Who else was willing to sacrifice his salvation for the children of Israel? Read Exodus 32:30-34.

While neither Paul nor Moses could literally give up his salvation for Israel, their desire showed a great love for their kinsmen and a concern for their eternal salvation. Ask the Lord to examine your heart. How concerned are you for the lost? What will you do about what the Lord reveals?

3.   Next Paul launches into a description of what it meant for the nation of Israel to be chosen by God. List what was included in the rich heritage of Israel? (v. 4-5)

Let's look at verse 5 in the NIV:

> *Theirs is the patriarchs, and from them is traced the human ancestry of Christ, who is God over all, forever praised! Amen.*

4.   How does Paul identify Jesus? What is the significance of his declaration?

Paul continued with the explanation that not all of Abraham's descendants are the true Israel. Does this mean that God's word has failed—that He did not keep His promises to Israel?

5.   If that were true, what would it mean to His faithfulness to the church?

6.   Read verses 6-13 and explain the difference between the children of the flesh and the children of promise.

7.   What is the basis for God's selection of the true Israel?

8. In verse 14, Paul asked the first of three rhetorical questions found in this chapter—there is no injustice with God, is there? How did Paul answer this question?

9. Upon what does God base His mercy?

Today we have just scratched the surface of Paul's discussion of God's sovereignty and human responsibility. These concepts have boggled the minds of many great theologians through the years. We will look into these concepts further tomorrow.

>>> FILLING UP WITH FAITH

What can we learn today in verse 5 or in the following Scriptures that could answer these potential questions from an unbeliever? Make notes on the details of the passages.

Is Jesus really God?

Colossians 2:9

Philippians 2:5-11

Hebrews 1:3

John 1:1

Did Jesus claim to be God?

John 8:58

John 10:30

John 10:36-38

Matthew 28:18

This is just a sampling of substantiating verses. There are many more passages that support the deity of Jesus—not to mention the miracles and the fulfillment of prophecy. You might take some time to investigate so that you can add even more to your resources.

Romans 9:19-33

In yesterday's lesson we read where Paul addressed the sovereignty of God by asking if God was unjust for choosing some to accomplish His purpose and rejecting others. He concluded that God is absolutely just in His dealings with mankind and further concluded that nothing is dependent on man but rather on God's mercy. With Paul's presentation on the sovereignty of God, the second rhetorical question in this chapter came to light in verse 19. *"Why does He still find fault? For who resists His will?"* In other words, if God is sovereign, how can anyone be held accountable for one could not resist God's will? Paul's response was to challenge the audacity of man questioning God. Did a creation possess more wisdom than the Creator? Then he interjected the illustration of the potter and the clay from both Isaiah and Jeremiah to prove his point.

1. Read the following passages and summarize.

    Isaiah 29:15-16

    Jeremiah 18:1-6

Paul reasoned that a holy God had the right and authority to use His creations to accomplish His purpose and had mentioned both Moses and Pharaoh earlier in this chapter to express this concept.

2. Using your knowledge of the account of the deliverance of Israel from Egypt (or refresh your memory with a quick glance at Exodus 1-12), compare Moses and Pharaoh, listing their station in life, etc.

Moses	Pharaoh

God had ordained both of these men to accomplish His plan. Both observed God's amazing miracles. Both were sinners, even murderers. Because God is longsuffering, both were given the opportunity to respond to God's mercy. They both had a choice. One chose mercy while the other chose judgment. Did either deserve mercy? Absolutely not. Thus, God is never unjust when He gives sinners what they deserve but He is ever gracious in extending mercy to the repentant. This brings us back to those seemingly conflicting concepts—the sovereignty of God and the responsibility of man. Perhaps this quote from the theologian, Warren Wiersbe, will be helpful to you.

> *No one will deny that there are many mysteries connected with divine sovereignty and human responsibility. Nowhere does God ask us to choose between these two truths, because they both come from God and are a part of God's plan. They do not compete; they cooperate. The fact that we cannot fully understand how they work together does not deny the fact that they do. When a man asked Charles Spurgeon how he reconciled divine sovereignty and human responsibility, Spurgeon replied: "I never try to reconcile friends!"[1]*

Next beginning in verse 22, Paul outlined God's provision for redemption and the establishment of His church by quoting Old Testament prophecies.

3. To whom were the prophecies referring in Hosea 2:23 and Hosea 1:10?

4. What did the prophet reveal concerning the Jews in the quote from Isaiah 10:22-23?

5. What would have been the ultimate fate of the Jews had God not left a remnant? (v. 29)

In verse 30, Paul asked the third question—What shall we say then?—and proceeded to compare the approach of the Jews and the Gentiles to a right relationship with God.

6. Contrast the Jews' and the Gentiles' approach toward righteousness. (vv. 30-32)

7. Why was Jesus a stumbling stone to the Jews?

So we see that God has been faithful to His word by fulfilling His prophecies—He did not cancel His covenant with the Jews, reserving a remnant, yet He graciously offered salvation to the Gentiles. And the church was born.

⫸ FILLING UP WITH FAITH

Is God unjust?

Another question that came up this week is whether God can be both loving and just in His relationship with mankind. Let's see what a few Scriptures say concerning God's justice. Make notes on what you read.

Deuteronomy 32:4

Psalm 89:14

Psalm 92:15

Daniel 4:37

Job 37:23

Zephaniah 3:5

This quote from Norman Geisler is a beautiful picture of the balance between God's justice and His love.

> God's justice demands that sin be punished, but his love compels him to save sinners. So by Christ's death for us his justice is satisfied and his love released. Thus, there is no contradiction between absolute justice and unconditional love. To illustrate, God is like the judge who, after passing out the punishment to the guilty defendant, laid aside his robe, stood alongside the convicted, and paid the fine for him. Jesus did the same for us on Calvary. Surely justice and mercy kissed at the cross.[12]

Romans 10:1-13

Paul began chapter 10 by again speaking of his intense desire that Israel might know true salvation from God. Yet, despite the fact of the promise of salvation by the Messiah found throughout their Scriptures, the Jewish people as a whole had rejected Jesus. They did not see their need of salvation. After all, they had the law—they were God's chosen people.

1. According to Paul what was lacking in the Jews' zeal for God?

2. What was the Jews' plan for securing righteousness?

3. Contrast righteousness based on the law and righteousness based on faith.

In verses 6-7, Paul quotes Deuteronomy 30:12-13 to prove his point that salvation by faith needed no human effort, no outward obedience, but rather a change of heart. This was the gist of a conversation I had with a young woman when I asked her exactly what it would take to be acceptable to God. Her response was typical—she said she believed that God would look at her life and weigh the good against the bad. She concluded with her belief that the good would outweigh the bad. I was then able to share with her—that's not really the way it works. And I started before the creation of the world and presented the truth of God's salvation plan. There is nothing—absolutely nothing—that can make our sinner's heart acceptable to a holy God. But God has made a way!

Paul proceeded to outline the way of salvation in verses 8-10. Using these verses as your guide, write a simple plan of salvation which you could share with an unbeliever.

Reflect on verses 11-13 from The Message.

> *Scripture reassures us, "No one who trusts God like this—heart and soul—will ever regret it." It's exactly the same no matter what a person's religious background may be: the same God for all of us, acting the same incredibly generous way to everyone who calls out for help. "Everyone who calls, 'Help, God!' gets help."*

4. Who may receive this gift of salvation? Memorize verse 13 if you have not already done so.

5. Whose salvation are you praying for now? Ask God to provide you an opportunity to share the way of salvation with him/her in the near future and to empower you to do it.

Paul then addressed the necessity of taking the gospel to the world in the very familiar passage in verses 14-17. There is a natural progression in the passage:

> *How will they call on Him in whom they have not believed?*
> *How will they believe in Him whom they have not heard?*
> *And how will they hear without a preacher?*
> *How will they preach unless they are sent?*

We are to go. We have been sent.

> *Go therefore and make disciples of all nations, baptizing them in the name of the Father and the Son and the Holy Spirit, teaching them to observe all that I commanded you; and lo, I am with you always, even to the end of the age.* Matthew 28:19-20

As we come to the end of chapter 10, we can almost hear the voice of the Apostle Paul as he reiterated these truths. Indeed, God offered Israel the gift of salvation—a simple process of belief and confession. Even though they had heard through the prophets of the Old Testament, eyewitness testimonies, and the preachers who had brought the news, they were a difficult and rebellious people and refused the gift rather choosing the law as their means of securing righteousness. Yet the Gentiles, who had not sought God, turned to Him accepting the salvation offered through Jesus Christ's death on the cross. Still, in love, God stretched out His hands to the Jews—despite their disobedience—because He is a covenant keeping God and He loves with an everlasting love.

Here is a question that today's lesson brings to mind.

Is Jesus the only way to God?

The following are some revealing quotations regarding the way our culture views the issue of the exclusiveness of Christianity as the way to peace with God.

> A major criticism leveled at Christians is that they have the arrogance to say Christianity is the only true religion and the only way to obtain eternal life. That view seems annoyingly exclusive and intolerant to most people. Consequently, most professed Christians in America no longer claim that Christianity is exclusive. A 2008 Pew Forum survey among Americans found that 65 percent of all professed Christians say there are multiple paths to eternal life, with 80 percent of the respondents citing at least one non-Christian religion that can lead to salvation.[13]

> Many people consider it arrogant, narrow-minded, and bigoted for Christians to contend that the only path to God must go through Jesus of Nazareth. In a day of religious pluralism and tolerance, this exclusivity claim is politically incorrect, a verbal slap in the face of other belief systems.[14]

While the culture we live in today may adhere to the above opinions, we as Christians have another authority. So let's look to see what the Bible has to say.

John 14:6

John 11:25-26

I Timothy 2:5-6a

Hebrews 10:19-22

If who Jesus claimed to be is true, then other religious claims cannot be true. See if you can locate other verses to use to answer an unbeliever's question.

Romans 11:1-15

As chapter 11 begins, Paul again addressed whether God had rejected His people, Israel. He answered with an emphatic no followed by a quote from the Old Testament narrative from the life of Elijah to prove his point that God had not turned His back on Israel. The scene took place after the conflict with the prophets of Baal on Mount Carmel. Although God had come down in power on his behalf, Elijah found himself discouraged as he evaded capture by Queen Jezebel and presented his case before the Lord.

1. Read the account from I Kings 19:9-18. What was God's response to Elijah's lament?

2. What did God promise Joshua as he succeeded Moses in Joshua 1:5b, 9?

All of Israel has never been totally faithful to the Lord but there has always been a remnant of those who were faithful to Him. And even when Israel was faithless, God remained faithful to them for He was not finished with Israel. So when Paul reminded the Romans that indeed there was a remnant of believers in Israel, it served as an encouragement to the church that God would also remain faithful to His church and His promises.

3. How does this encouragement to believers resonate with you?

4. Think about a time when your problems seemed insurmountable and you felt all alone. Did you take your problems to the Lord? If so, how did God reveal Himself to you?

5. Upon what were the Israelites to base their salvation? (v. 6)

6. Upon what had they relied in the past?

7. What was the result? (vs. 7-10)

The gift of grace is absolutely unfathomable to our minds. Perhaps that is why Israel continued to seek righteousness and standing with God through works. Yet God evaluated man's righteousness in Isaiah 64:6a, "For all of us have become like one who is unclean, and all our righteous deeds are like a filthy garment." Nothing could bridge that gap between a holy God and sinful man aside from grace.

8. What happened because of Israel's rejection of Jesus? (v. 11)

9. What did Paul, the apostle to the Gentiles, hope that the salvation of the Gentiles would create in the Jews?

Though the gospel came to the Gentiles because of the rejection of the Jews, God's commitment to a relationship with the Jews has never wavered. He will not break His covenant as stated in the following passage from the prophet, Jeremiah.

> *Thus says the Lord, who gives the sun for light by day and the fixed order of the moon and the stars for light by night, who stirs up the sea so that its waves roar; the Lord of hosts is His name: "If this fixed order departs from before Me," declares the Lord, "then the offspring of Israel also will cease from being a nation before Me forever." Thus says the Lord, "If the heavens above can be measured and the foundations of the earth searched out below, then I will also cast off all the offspring of Israel for all that they have done," declares the Lord.* Jeremiah 31:33-37

Thus saith the Lord and that settles it.

>>> FILLING UP WITH FAITH

In a culture where keeping your word seems to have become a discarded virtue, a seeker might be skeptical that God, if He exists, could be trusted to fulfill His promises. So it is important for us to acquire a firm scriptural foundation regarding the reliability of God when asked the following question.

Is God faithful to keep His promises?

Scripture is full of reminders of God's faithfulness to Israel from the call of Abraham—to the birth of Isaac—to the deliverance from Egypt—to their arrival in the Promised Land—to the return from captivity—to the birth of the Messiah—to their reestablishment in their land in 1948 as the nation of Israel. By merely reviewing the history of Israel, how could we ever doubt God's faithfulness to his promises?

Record your impressions from these passages.

Remember His faithfulness is constant and enduring:

    Lamentations 3:23

    Psalm 89:33

    Hebrews 10:23

    2 Corinthians 1:20

Count on His faithfulness in these situations:

    When you are faithless
    2 Timothy 2:13

    When you face temptation
    1 Corinthians 10:13

    When you need forgiveness
    1 John 1:9

    When you need protection
    2 Thessalonians 3:3

GOD IS FAITHFUL!

Romans 11:16-36

Paul sustained his familiar theme as he continued his treatise of God's faithfulness to Israel by referencing the Lord's instructions regarding the contribution offering once they entered the Promised Land. Found in Numbers 15, the Israelites were to offer a loaf of dough in thanksgiving for the Lord's provision of a good harvest. Paul reasoned that if the first piece of the loaf was holy therefore the whole loaf was holy. Then he referred to the olive tree, the symbol for the nation Israel, making mention that if the root was holy then the branches were as well. So what did Paul mean here? In essence, because of the covenant God had made with Abraham, even though not all of Israel accepted the Messiah, it still maintained its place in God's plan. Though some of the branches of the olive tree were broken off, He was not finished with Israel.

1. What warning did Paul have for the Gentile Christians? (v. 18)

2. Why were the natural branches broken off?

3. What enabled the wild branches to be grafted in?

4. How could be the natural branches be grafted back into the tree?

5. In verses 25-26, Paul made an amazing revelation that had previously been hidden. What did he reveal?

Let's wrap our minds around what Paul said—all Israel will be saved when the full number of the Gentiles has been completed. Paul declared that the hardening of the Jews was only temporary and a future national conversion of Israel would take place when Jesus returns. Though not every Jew has trusted in God's redemption plan through the centuries, one day they will see Him as whom He is.

6. Read Zechariah 12:10. How will the Jews someday view Jesus?

In verse 29, the Scripture says, "for the gifts and the calling of God are irrevocable." This reiterated what Paul had been saying throughout these three chapters we have studied this week. It is a recurrent theme in God's dealings with the children of Israel. We can rest in the confidence that He is a covenant keeping God and we can depend on His promises.

7. Read Deuteronomy 7:7-9. Make a list of the things that are revealed about God in this passage.

8. How were you encouraged in your faith by what you read?

Paul was so encouraged by the mere reflection of God's amazing grace to Jew and Gentile alike that he broke out into a doxology—praising Him for His wisdom and knowledge, His judgments, and His ways. Could we possibly do any less?

Reflect on this final verse of Chapter 11 and how it defines your understanding of our Mighty God.

For from Him and through Him and to Him are all things. To Him be the glory forever. Amen.

Reflecting on Paul's praise of our Great God at the end of Chapter 11 brings another question to mind frequently asked by seekers.

Is it possible to know God?

How can we possibly begin to explain the intricacies of God? Surely He is both incomprehensible and knowable. Perhaps the following quotes will shed some light on this seemingly conflicting concept.

> Scripture teaches that we can have a true and personal knowledge of God, but this does not mean we will ever understand him exhaustively. The Bible is clear that God is ultimately incomprehensible to us; that is, we can never fully comprehend his whole being.[15]

> The incomprehensibility of God could lead to despair or apathy in the quest to know God, but the Bible also teaches that God is knowable. While God can never be exhaustively understood, he can be known truly, personally, and sufficiently. God is personal, has definite characteristics, and has personally revealed himself so he can be truly known.[16]

Read the following Scriptures and record what they say about the incomprehensibility or the knowability of God.

Psalm 145:3

Isaiah 55:8-9

2 Peter 1:2-3

Jeremiah 9:23-24

What we know about God affects what we believe about God. In turn, we live out those very beliefs and share them through our actions with the world. Rather than treating the study of God as a luxury item with too high a price tag for our intellect and our time, we must hunger for knowledge of God and strive for it as the ultimate necessity for survival, more essential than the very food we eat.[17]

WEEK EIGHT

Clinging to the Good

Let love be without hypocrisy. Abhor what is evil; cling to what is good.
Romans 12:9

Generally, Paul began his letters with an exposition of doctrine to inform his readers about the vast riches of their inheritance in Christ. Then once he completed that message, he followed with the practical application of those truths to the Christian life. And true to his usual form, in Romans, once he elaborated on doctrinal issues and the defense of the faithfulness of God, Paul moved on to encourage his readers in practical scriptural living. And he started the chapter by suggesting a sacrifice. Wait a minute you say— wasn't the age of sacrifice concluded with Jesus' once and for all sacrifice on the cross? Let's delve into the passage and see.

⫸ DAY ONE ⫷

Romans 12:1

The concept of sacrifice was first found in Genesis in the narrative about Cain and Abel. God accepted one sacrifice and rejected the other.

1. Read Genesis 4:3-8. Why was Cain's sacrifice unacceptable?

2. What warning did God give Cain? How did he respond to the situation?

As God developed the sacrificial system with the Children of Israel, He had strict guidelines as to what would constitute an acceptable sacrifice.

3. What instructions do you find in the following verses regarding an acceptable sacrifice?

    Leviticus 22:19

    Deuteronomy 17:1

The very nature of our God is holiness and righteousness and He cannot abide sin in His presence thus we understand His requirement for a pure and perfect sacrifice. Yet we know that the sin of Adam and Eve in the Garden of Eden left us all with the inherited sin nature of Adam. But we remember that God in His mercy and love did not leave us in that lost estate but provided a remedy for us in His Son, our Lord Jesus Christ.

4. Review Hebrews 9:24-28. What did our High Priest do for us?

5. Read Hebrews 10:12. What did Jesus do that no earthly priest could?

6. How did His action affect our relationship with a Holy God?

So it seems only fitting that we might ruminate on Paul's encouragement to the believers in verse 1 to present their bodies as a living and holy sacrifice to God. We can present ourselves on the altar as a pure and spotless sacrifice. Obviously, not because of anything we have done but in light of what Jesus did for us on the cross. We are covered with His robe of righteousness—we are acceptable to God.

7. Reflect on these passages and rejoice.

    Isaiah 61:10

    2 Corinthians 5:21

In this passage, Paul instructed the believers to be living sacrifices. How is that possible? All the animals in the Old Testament sacrifices died. Another option is available to mankind however when we trust Jesus to pay the penalty for our sin and provide His righteous covering for us. It is called life. Jesus is alive and so are believers—perfectly prepared to become a living sacrifice if we but choose. How could we do any less after all He has done for us? It is a choice to die to self and to live in obedience to Him.

Let's commit to daily presenting ourselves as living sacrifices, holy and acceptable—*which is your spiritual service of worship.*

Today we have talked about the holiness of God and the sinfulness of man which leads us to a question that you might hear from a seeker.

Why did Jesus need to die?

To understand the necessity of a sacrifice in order for mankind to have access to God, we need to contemplate His very nature. Two of the attributes we should consider are His holiness and His love which play into His divine design for redemption. Read the following passages to discover where God's holiness and His love met.

God's Holiness

Exodus 15:11

Revelation 15:4

God's Love

Ephesians 2:4-5

1 John 4:9-10

Let this quote by Josh and Sean McDowell ruminate in your mind and create an attitude of thanksgiving for God's great mercy and love.

> So what was God to do? He couldn't have a relationship with humans as they were, because of sin—that would violate his holiness and purity. He couldn't overlook sin and say, "Oh, that's okay—I'll let bygones be bygones." That would violate his justice. But if he did nothing humans would remain eternally separated from him.
>
> God's holiness couldn't abide sin and his justice couldn't overlook it. Yet his love couldn't stand by and do nothing. So he devised a masterful and merciful plan. But it would cost him dearly—the death of his only Son.[18]

The sacrifice was beyond understanding. Thank you Lord Jesus!

Romans 12:2

As I write this study, it is the night of the presidential election. I haven't heard any of the news reports yet, but as I reflect on these last months of campaigning and the various issues that have come to the forefront, I couldn't help but smile at the appropriateness of our study for today. Sometimes I think our culture has gone mad—who would have dreamed of the enormous changes that have taken place in our country in the last fifty years—abortion, same-sex marriage, the overwhelming preponderance of drug abuse, situational ethics, and I could go on and on. As Christians we have a choice to make—to live in sync with the culture or to live counter-culturally. And that is what our study is about today.

1. Read Romans 12:2. What instructions did Paul give to the Christians in Rome?

2. Look up the words conform and transform in the dictionary and write the definitions below.

3. Do you find it difficult to live counter-culturally? If so, why?

In his letter to Timothy, Paul described the last days and it sounds eerily familiar to the times in which we live.

4. Review this passage from 2 Timothy 3:1-5. What advice does Paul give Timothy?

Unfortunately, faulty thinking can filter into the church, as well, when culture creeps in. Paul warned Timothy to be on the lookout for it.

5. In 2 Timothy 4:3-4, what warning did Paul give to Timothy concerning the church? Explain any evidence you have seen reflective of these verses in the church today?

Paul gave us a hint on how to live counter-culturally—the renewing of your mind. This renewal is absolutely crucial to Christ-like living. We can live our life as a conformer imitating the world or as a transformer imitating Christ. The choice is ours.

> Our minds contain deeply held beliefs and attitudes which have been learned through our environment, experiences, and education. These beliefs and attitudes produce thoughts which reflect how we perceive the events in our lives. These thoughts, then, combined with past experiences, relationships, and patterns of behavior, are often the source of our emotions, and our emotions are usually the launching pad for our actions.[19]

> Many of our thoughts can be traced back to our beliefs—beliefs which are either founded on the truths of Scripture, or the lies of Satan.[20]

6. Read Proverbs 23:7a. Why is what you think important?

7. Through prayerful, honest evaluation, determine who or what controls your thinking. Is there any action that needs to take place following your evaluation?

Paul delivered some advice to the church at Colossae concerning the renewal of their minds. He urged them to think with an eternal focus.

8. What does Paul encourage the Christians to do in Colossians 3:1-3? What reason does he give for the ability to walk through life with an eternal perspective?

Bolstered by a new thinking pattern, we can walk counter-culturally through our life. But it is never easy. The enemy and even our own flesh sends us messages that would drag us off course. Yet even though we are in the midst of this battle, as Christians, we have weapons at our disposal.

9. Read 2 Corinthians 10:3-5. Outline the steps in this passage for taking every thought captive.

With a renewed mind, we are enabled to interpret God's will for us—His "good, acceptable and perfect will."

⋙ FILLING UP WITH FAITH

Today we have reflected upon walking counter-culturally in our world. As we interact with others, we will find that frequently the biblical view of truth conflicts with what others believe. So you might hear the following question from an unbeliever.

Why do Christians want to impose their values and view of truth on me?

In a pluralistic society, everyone's values are viewed as equally valid thus it doesn't matter what you believe as long as you are sincere. What we believe about life composes our worldview which influences how we live our life.

> Whether conscious or subconscious, every person has some type of worldview. A personal worldview is a combination of all you believe to be true, and what you believe becomes the driving force behind every emotion, decision and action. Therefore, it affects your response in every area of life.

> A biblical worldview is based on the infallible Word of God. When you believe the Bible is entirely true, then you allow it to be the foundation of everything you say and do. Nonbiblical worldview ideas don't just sit in a book somewhere waiting for people to examine them. They bombard us constantly from television, film, music, newspapers, magazines, books and academia.

> Because we live in a selfish, fallen world, these ideas seductively appeal to the desires of our flesh, and we often end up incorporating them into our personal worldview. Sadly, we often do this without even knowing it.[21]

If we say we know the truth and do not share it with others then we have failed. Our job is not to cram it down the throats of unbelievers but to lovingly, gently share what we know both from God's Word and experientially. Explore these verses to discover what they say about truth, worldview, and life. Record what you learn and be prepared to share it with others.

Ephesians 4:1

Micah 6:8

Colossians 2:6-8

Ephesians 4:17-18

Romans 12:3-8

After Paul's discourse on becoming a living sacrifice and renewing your mind, he developed the concept of the church as the body of Christ empowered by spiritual gifts. But before he launched into that, Paul reminded the church members of a potential pitfall—the sin of pride.

1. What admonition did Paul give in verse 3? What would be the result of such a lack of judgment?

2. What is God's opinion of pride based on the following Scriptures?

    Proverbs 6:16-19 (NKJV)

    Proverbs 26:12

    Proverbs 28:25

Obviously, Paul understood the temptation to exalt oneself as opposed to thinking in terms of the whole body of Christ with different but equally valuable functions.

3. Read Romans 12:4-5 and 1 Corinthians 12:12-24 and give a synopsis of Paul's explanation of the concept of the body of Christ.

4. Review 1 Corinthians 12:25-26 and describe Paul's purpose in his lengthy explanation of God's plan for body life.

Paul outlined the role of spiritual gifts for the edification of the body of Christ, a new concept to believers, both in Romans 12 and 1 Corinthians 12. In the Old Testament, we have seen illustrations of the anointing of the Holy Spirit but not the infilling. What a wonderful blessing to the believer—God indwelling you.

5. What did Jesus reveal about the Holy Spirit to the disciples in John 14:26 and John 16:7-15?

6. Relate what happened on the Day of Pentecost when the Holy Spirit fell on the church as recorded in Acts 2:1-4.

As Paul developed the explanation of the spiritual gifts, he answered a couple of questions the believers might have had.

7. Read 1 Corinthians 12:7, 11. What was the purpose of spiritual gifts and who determines each individual's gift?

8. Using the passages from Romans 12:6-8 and 1 Corinthians 12:8-10, record the spiritual gifts listed on the chart.

SPIRITUAL GIFTS

Romans 12	1 Corinthians 12

9. Have you discovered your spiritual gift/gifts? If so, how are you using it to edify the body of Christ? If not, go to this link: http://www.bellevue.org/next-step-classes#discover.

You are gifted! Make it your lifestyle to share your gift with others.

⫸ FILLING UP WITH FAITH

The study of the Holy Spirit and spiritual gifts brings up a question that you might be asked.

Do Christians have three Gods?

Perhaps one of the most confusing elements in understanding God is the concept that He is triune.

> God being a Trinity does not mean there are three Gods. God exists as three persons, yet he is one being. Each person of the Trinity—the Father, the Son and the Holy Spirit—has separate identity while yet possessing the full nature of God.[22]

Reflect on the following Scriptures revealing both the oneness and the distinctiveness of God. Record what you find.

Deuteronomy 6:4

Isaiah 45:5-6

John 1:1-2

John 14:26

1 Peter 1:2

Jude 20-21

2 Corinthians 13:14

While it is difficult to wrap our minds around the Trinity—a God that is one yet three—it reinforces what we concluded earlier in this study that God is incomprehensible yet knowable.

Romans 12:9-16

As Paul continued with the practical application of living out life as a believer, he presented several imperatives in this passage. While not directly related, they all comprise a mandate for relationships with other believers.

1. Make a list of the imperatives mentioned in this passage.

While we are unable to study each one of the imperatives, we will highlight two starting with love.

2. Read 1 Corinthians 13:4-8a and list the attributes of love.

3. What commands did Jesus give us concerning love in John 15:12 and 1 Corinthians 16:14?

4. As you read Colossians 3:12-14, compare Paul's instructions to getting dressed. After adding each garment, what would be your coat—that final piece? What does Paul call it?

5. How would our relationships be different if we covered everything with love?

Hatred stirs up strife, but love covers all transgressions. Proverbs 10:12

If love is to be our goal, we can assume that the source for that abounding love must flow out of a heart of humility. So let's take a look at the definition of humility through the example of Jesus.

6. Read Philippians 2:1-4. How does Paul define humility in this passage?

7. From Philippians 2:5-8, describe Jesus' example of humility.

The content from our Romans passage today seems to emphasize the necessity for humility as it presents the guidelines for our relationships with others.

8. Glance back over the Scripture for today and record all the guidelines that necessitate humility.

9. Review the following verses to determine God's regard for humility and record it.

   Psalm 138:6

   Proverbs 29:23

   Isaiah 57:15

God has given us a mandate to serve one another in humility and love. Of course, this can be challenging with those we love dearly much less those sand paper people that God allows in our lives. Living it out in our day to day lives can be challenging but remember we have the empowering Holy Spirit to help us carry it out.

10. How are you doing in the area of loving others with a heart of humility? What steps can you take to doing it with abandon?

Therefore I, the prisoner of the Lord, implore you to walk in a manner worthy of the calling with which you have been called with all humility and gentleness, with patience, showing tolerance for one another in love, being diligent to preserve the unity of the Spirit in the bond of peace. Ephesians 4:1-3

Today we have looked at walking in right relationship with others. To live in this manner takes a goodness that can only be explained through the new birth and walking in the Spirit. Left to our own devices, we all tend to be self-consumed rather than others-focused. Yet amazingly, people tend to think that they can be good on their own which leads us to our apologetic question for today.

Won't God just look at my life and weigh the good against the bad to let me into heaven?

Because God is holy and mankind is sinful, this premise will not work to produce eternal life. Once sin entered into the life of the first man, Adam, all mankind inherited a sinful nature. The presence of but one sin is enough to prevent one from entering into the joys of heaven. Scripture is very clear about our fallen estate. Peruse the following Scriptures to observe and record what God has to say.

Job 25:4

Ecclesiastes 7:20

1 Corinthians 6:9a

Still man has the mistaken opinion that he can either deny his sin or provide a remedy of his own.

I John 1:10

Proverbs 20:9

Jeremiah 2:22

But God has made a way and His name is Jesus.

John 1:29

Ephesians 1:7

Rejoice that your name is written in heaven!

Romans 12:14, 17-21

Yesterday we contemplated building strong relationships within the church. In contrast, today we will focus on living in peace even with our enemies. Since we live in a fallen world populated by sinners, most of us could relate a story of a deep personal hurt. When such a wound has been perpetrated on us, then, we have a sober decision to make—what will we choose—blessings or cursing—forgiveness or revenge. The choice is ours but the decision should be made in light of Scripture.

1. Record Jesus' instructions concerning our enemies from the following verses.

   Matthew 5:43-44

   Luke 6:27-35

   Luke 17:3-4

Perhaps you are thinking—but you don't know what that person did to me or someone I love. I can't let it go—the hurt is too deep. Yet all of us have offended a holy God. Let's think about what He has done for us.

2. Review the following passages for a reminder of what God has done for you. Record what you find.

   Psalm 103:10-12

   Romans 5:6-8

   Colossians 3:13

   Micah 7:8-9

3. Many throughout Scripture chose to forgive even when the cost was great. Here are three examples. Make comments on what you glean from these verses.

   Joseph—Genesis 50:15-21

   Stephen—Acts 7:54-60

   Jesus—Luke 23:34

Years ago, I watched my husband live out forgiveness in a very devastating situation and it made an indelible impression on me. He chose to love when it would have been much easier to hate—to reach out rather than to ignore—to show kindness when he had been treated unkindly—to pray rather than to curse.

Jesus instructed us to love our enemies and to forgive them. He also beautifully demonstrated it for us. But it can be difficult to put it into practice. In our flesh, we want revenge. As Paul concluded chapter 12 of Romans, he addressed this issue quoting from Deuteronomy and Proverbs.

4. Read Romans 12:17-21. What do the verses say about taking revenge?

5. Based on Proverbs 20:22, when tempted to get revenge, what should we do?

6. What bit of advice did Paul give us in 1 Thessalonians 5:15?

Paul encouraged us to practice forgiveness, to avoid vengefulness, and to live in peace. Based on what we have studied today, we have the formula and in the power of the Holy Spirit, we can do it.

Depart from evil and do good; Seek peace and pursue it. Psalm 34:14

Since we discussed the necessity of forgiveness today, a question comes to light that we need to be prepared to answer.

Where did evil come from?

While there is much discussion in our society about what constitutes good and evil, the vast majority would certainly agree that evil does exist. The explanation given by Josh and Sean McDowell is very enlightening.

> God is perfectly good and holy and created only perfect creatures. Yet he gave his human creation the power of free choice or free will. The first humans had a choice to trust in him, to believe that he was good and that he had their best interest at heart when he gave them a command to obey. Unfortunately they used this good power to choose against him, and that brought evil into this world.
>
> Of course God could have created a world without free will. Humans could have been "programmed" to do good and worship him perfectly. Yet in a world without choices the true meaning of "I love you" would be lost. The fulfilling purpose and reality of loving another is void and meaningless without the power to freely choose. God wanted us to experience the reality of a love relationship together with him. The great risk was the possibility of evil. And the great responsibility to act on that possibility rested with humans, not God.[23]

Evil was first introduced in the Garden of Eden.

Genesis 3:1-7

We saw it again in the murder of Abel.

Genesis 4:1-10

God judged it with the flood.

Genesis 6:5

And on and on it went. But God has a plan to alleviate evil once and for all.

Revelation 21:1-4

Jesus paid the penalty for evil.

Colossians 1:21-2

WEEK NINE
Get Dressed!

But put on the Lord Jesus Christ, and make no provision
for the flesh in regard to its lusts.
Romans 13:14

Romans 13 - 14

As we saw last week, the redemptive relationship we have with Jesus Christ impacts every other relationship in our lives. As Paul concluded Romans 12, he gave instructions regarding the way Christians should relate to unbelieving family members, neighbors, and employers. In Romans 13, he explains the way believers should relate to the government.

Keep in mind, Paul is writing to the church in Rome, the capital city of the Roman Empire. Living as a Christian in A.D. 57 was not an easy time. Paul and the recipients of his letter lived under a brutal regime that is still renowned for its calloused inhumanity. At the time Paul was penning his letter to the church in Rome, the tax burden was so heavy that pockets of resistance were beginning to form. Add to that the doubt and mistrust that shrouded the government's view of Christians. For example, those who professed to follow Christ were often suspected of sedition. Just a few years earlier, when Paul had visited Thessalonica, those who opposed him accused him of "acting against the decrees of Caesar, saying that there is another king, Jesus." Acts 17:7 ESV

In addition, Christians were often blamed and persecuted for causing socio-economic disruptions. Business owners, like Demetrius the silversmith (see Acts 19), who depended upon religion for their livelihood, were threatened by Christians who not only had no need for the idols they propagated, but who were also preaching and teaching against idol worship period.

Couple this political backdrop with the possibility that some believers might have interpreted his command to avoid conformity with the world (12:2) as permission to rebel against the authority of Rome, and we get a sense of why Paul is writing to the believers in Rome instructing them on how to live during these times.

Romans 13:1-7

One of the areas where they needed direction was how to relate to the government. The first seven verses in Romans 13 are the most noteworthy instructions in the New Testament regarding civic responsibility. Paul minces no words as he delves into the topic of how believers are to relate to governing authorities. Plain and simple, we are to be in subjection. The word subjection is defined as "one who is under the rule of another or others, especially one who owes allegiance to a government or ruler."[24]

1. Take a moment and list some of the "governing authorities" in our culture.

2. Who established these authorities in our lives (vv. 1-4)?

Another translation of the Greek term "be in subjection" in verse 1 is "submit" (see James 4:7 and I Peter 2:13). Submission conveys the picture of a person yielding his or her will to a higher power. Paul knew that the believers in Rome needed to exercise care to live peaceably within the structure of the Roman Empire and resist the urge to complain or join the groundswell of zealot rebellion already simmering against the authoritarian rule of the state. Paul uses the term "be in subjection," rather than the more forceful word, "obey." Being in subjection or submitting is an attitude of the heart. On the other hand, obedience is an action, an unwavering, rigid adherence.

3. What are some of the practical differences between submit and obey?

4. In the Bible, there were times when God's people disobeyed the base political structure of the day. One example of God's faithful objecting to the requirements of the government is found in Daniel 3:1-30. What command did Shadrach, Meshach, and Abednego refuse to obey?

5. How did God honor them through King Nebuchadnezzar (vv. 28-30)?

In the New Testament, we read in Acts 5 where Peter made a similar stand in Jerusalem. After performing miracles throughout the area, Peter and the other apostles were arrested due to the jealousy of the high priest and his associates. The night of their arrest, an angel appeared and freed them from jail to go back and preach in the temple once again. Their perseverance infuriated the captain of the temple guard and the chief priests who then took them to the Sanhedrin to be tried. In verse 28 the high priest accused, "We gave you strict orders not to preach in this name (Jesus), and yet, you have filled Jerusalem with your teaching and intend to bring this man's blood upon us."

6. How did Peter and the apostles answer this accusation in verse 29?

7a. What are some possible instances when a believer might not be able to obey the government today?

7b. In such a case, what attitude should a Christian have toward governing authority?

Although there were and are occasions when a Christian has to make the choice to "obey God rather than men," Paul makes it clear to the Roman Christians and to us that it is God's will to govern mankind through human authorities.

7. Read 1 Peter 2:13. Why should a believer submit to governing structures in society?

8. In verses Romans 13:2-4, Paul gives a stern warning to believers who choose to rebel against authority. What is the motivation Paul gives for obeying the government?

9. What are some examples of times when a believer should obey the law out of a spirit of submission, even if he or she does not want to do so?

10. In verses 5-7, Paul moves to a different level of motivation in regards to obedience—conscience. In what practical area does he say a believer should obey in order to maintain a clear conscience?

Romans 13:8-14

Yesterday, we closed our study with an explanation of what we owe to those who are over us in the established hierarchy of order that God has ordained for our protection. Beginning with Romans 13:8, Paul transitions his discourse to what we owe others. Very simply, his answer can be reduced to one word...love. This is a continuing theme. Last week, in Chapter 12, we saw where Paul exhorted believers to exercise their spiritual gifts in love. In the verses we are diving into today, we will find that love is a blanket that we should use to cover all of our interactions with others. Later this week, in Chapter 14, we will see how love relates to our personal convictions.

Throughout Paul's writings, he shows believers the practical ways that they can express their faith to an unbelieving world. It is vital to realize, though, that every demonstration of faith never wanders far from the shadow of the Great Commandment.

1. Read Mark 12:28-31 and personalize the implications of these two commands, making sure to consider the correlation between the two.

2. How does Paul define love in Romans 13:8-10?

Biblical love is not an emotion; it is a mindset, which insinuates it is something we have to set our minds to do. The love Paul is talking about is a deliberate choice that requires intentionality and discipline. We are to love when we don't feel like it, love even if our flesh opposes the very notion of the thought, and love whether the object of our action is capable of reception or reciprocity.

3. Who is our neighbor, the object of our love that Paul refers to in verses 8-10? (See Luke 10:25-37 for a reminder of Jesus' definition of the word.)

> Do not waste time bothering whether you 'love' your neighbor; act as if you did. As soon as we do this we find one of the great secrets. When you are behaving as if you loved someone, you will presently come to love him.[25]

In verse 10, Paul clarifies that love supersedes every other law. So, whether we have a legal responsibility to do so or not, our response to others should always be love.

4. Read James 2:8-9, James 4:11, and I Peter 2:16-17. What are some practical ways that we can demonstrate the law of love?

Reading today's passage, you can hear the urgency in Paul's voice, the intensity in his teaching. In verse 11, he explains the reason for his resolve--the time for Christ's return is near.

5. Take a moment and think back over the last 24 hours in your life. Sifting your actions through the sieve of the imminent return of Christ, what would you have done differently?

In verses 12-14, Paul uses the imagery of night and day to differentiate the lifestyle of believers from that of non-believers. In Scripture, day and light epitomize all that opposes night and dark. Paul writes in Ephesians 5:8, "for you were formerly darkness, but now you are Light in the Lord; walk as children of Light."

6. In 1 Peter 2:11, Peter warns believers that fleshly lusts will "wage war against the soul." As children of the Light, what are some of the things that believers must lay down in order to make "no provision for the flesh" (13:14)?

7. What does it mean to put on the Lord Jesus Christ (v.14)? Read Galatians 3:27, Ephesians 4:24, and Colossians 3:10,12 for a fuller understanding of what Paul is saying.

⟫⟫⟫ FILLING UP WITH FAITH

Is God Legalistic?

One question, in particular, might arise from reading today's passage: If love fulfills the law, do we still have to obey the law?

God gave us the law for our protection and provision. His ways are the path to blessing and life. His commands are for our good. His motivation is not about the rules. His reasoning is all about His relationship with us.

Read the following passages and record the benefits of staying within the boundaries God has set for us.

Deuteronomy 30:15-21

Jeremiah 29:11

John 15:10-11

Romans 14:1-7

Conflict. Disagreements. Differing Opinions. These issues exist in marriages, families, the workplace, and yes, the church. Paul knew the damage divisiveness would bring into the fragile organization of the early church. In Romans 14, Paul counsels believers on the importance of maintaining unity in their midst and the need to embrace each other's differences.

To understand the points of contention within the early church, it will be helpful to examine the demographic make-up of the body. Throughout the book of Romans, Paul has been addressing the macro-difference in the church—Jewish believers vs. Gentile believers. But, there were also micro-differences that were threatening harmony. Some members were slaves; others were masters. Some were rich; still more were poor. Some were mature in their faith; others were still in the milk drinking early days of their newfound faith in Christ.

1. How were those who are "weak in faith" to be treated (v. 1)?

The Greek word for "accept" can also be translated "receive" or "welcome". Paul directs the church to exercise intentional, unconditional hospitality and acceptance in their fellowship, regardless of position, personal preference, or place on the spiritual growth chart. He challenges believers to view their differences as an opportunity to learn and grow.

2. What are some of the "opinions" (NASB) and "disputable matters" (NIV), the hot button issues, within the church today (v.1)?

Welcome with open arms fellow believers who don't see things the way you do. And don't jump all over them every time they say or do something you don't agree with.
Romans 14:1 (MSG)

In verse 2, Paul gives some insight into one of the issues that was causing rumblings within the church. This melting pot of believers had diverse views regarding dietary practices. Some of the Jewish Christians still took special care with their food preparation and turned up their noses when their Gentile brothers and sisters ate a ham sandwich. Others had no problem benefiting from the discount price on meat that had been offered in pagan ritual sacrifice (See 1 Corinthians 8-9). However, those Gentiles who had been delivered from a past of idol worship had real issues with eating "previously used" meat.

3. What instruction does Paul give to church regarding the differences that existed among them (v.3)?

In things necessary, unity; in things not necessary, liberty; in all things, grace.[26]

4. In verse 4, Paul quickly gets to the heart of the matter concerning the non-essentials. It is accountability. Who holds believers accountable regarding Christian liberties (matters upon which there is no clear scriptural teaching)?

In verses 5-6, Paul ventures to discuss another hot topic in the early church: the observation of holidays, Jewish or pagan. Gentiles did not appreciate the Sabbath or other Jewish holy days the way the Jews thought they should. To the Christian from a Gentile background, holidays reminded them of celebrations for pagan gods, festivals that "exchanged the truth of God for a lie, and worshipped and served the creature, rather than the Creator" (Romans 1:25). When Jewish Christians celebrated a holiday, it reminded Gentile believers of their idolatrous former life. Both groups frustrated each other! Diets and days were becoming a distraction within the body, fracturing the ability of the body to live in "one accord." Acts 1:14

5. Read the following verses that speak to unity within the church and summarize their meaning.

Philippians 2:2

1 Corinthians 1:10

2 Corinthians 13:11

I Peter 3:8

6. Paul gives a rule of thumb for believers regarding non-moral, non-scriptural differences in verse 5. What does it mean for "every person to be convinced in his (or her) own mind"?

7. Has there been an issue like this that you have had to grapple with in your own life? If so, how did you resolve it? What specific scriptures did God use to refine or redefine what you believed?

8. How should the reality of verse 7 impact our relationships with others and bring resolution to some of our intra-church differences?

⫸ FILLING UP WITH FAITH

Is some truth personal preference?

To answer this question, the difference between truth and belief must be examined. The truth, what God says, is autonomous from our beliefs. So, while we may have some individual, personal beliefs, the truth is the same for everyone. In the passage we have looked at today, Paul was saying that there are some matters outside the moral law of God (truth) that require a believer to make a personal decision.

What are some non-compromising truths to which all believers must subscribe?

List 3-4 examples of areas where a believer has the freedom to make a personal decision.

Romans 14:8-12

One of the hazards Christians face is trying to hurry up the work God is doing in the life of another believer. As we saw yesterday, judging is one of the manipulative tools that Christians use. This tendency to play Holy Spirit steps outside of the order God has set in place. Believers belong to God, not one another. God is in charge. He controls the transformation process in other believers. Trying to alter another person's behavior can interfere with the work God is trying to do in that individual's life. The work is His alone to do.

1. Read Ephesians 2:10. How does Paul describe a believer in this verse?

Another word for "workmanship" is masterpiece. It is the Greek word, "poiema" from which we get the word, "poem". Each of us is a God-designed original. In the space below, journal your response to the realization that you are one of His prized possessions.

In Romans 14:8, Paul emphasizes that our lives, from the moment of conception to death, belong to God. We live to Him and die to Him.

2. Transitioning this thought from our relationship with the Lord to our relationship with other believers, do we treat them as though they also belong to the Lord? Or do we try to rule their lives?

3. Read verses 9-10 and explain the reason believers are not to judge each other.

Judging others in the context that Paul uses the word in verses 10-12 contains no positive element. It does not build up, encourage, or seek to see transformation. Only God has the right to appraise the value of a person.

4. In verse 10, Paul explains that all believers will stand before the judgment seat of Christ. Read the verses below and summarize what that day will be like for a believer.

   2 Corinthians 5:10

   Matthew 12:36

   1 Peter 4:5

   James 1:12

5. In verse 11, Paul quotes the prophet Isaiah to describe the day when believers will see the Lord (Is. 45:23). What unifying posture will every believer assume on that day?

6. Read Philippians 2:10-11 and Psalm 95:6 and record additional details of what heaven will look (and sound) like that day.

There are times when we may also have to defend the faith to believers. One question a believer might ask after reading today's passage is:

Since believers have been saved from the penalty of sin, why will they be judged on Judgment Day?

When Christ returns, everyone's life will be assessed. On that day, Matthew 25:31-46 clearly states that Jesus will separate the sheep (believers) from the goats (unbelievers) and hold them accountable for their actions. Although a Christian's eternal destiny is secure, Jesus will evaluate a believer's life and reward them accordingly.

Read verses 34-40 in Matthew 25 and note some of the ways believers will be judged by Jesus.

Romans 14:13-23

At the beginning of this chapter, Paul cautioned believers against constructing barriers that would exclude weaker Christians from their fellowship. In Romans 14:13-23, Paul encourages them to process all of their actions and choices through the filter of brotherly love. As the church combines an attitude of acceptance and love with biblical instruction, the ensuing atmosphere will embolden younger, weaker Christians to flourish and mature.

1. Read verses 13-15. What are some of the ways that Christians can have a negative impact on each other?

In a similar discussion with the Corinthian church, Paul notes, "Now about food sacrificed to idols: We know that 'We all possess knowledge.' But knowledge puffs up while love builds up" (1 Corinthians 8:1). Knowledge that is not coupled with love can harm young believers; knowledge intertwined with love yields growth.

2. What are some biblical examples of ways mature Christians can teach weaker Christians in love? (Note the scripture as well as the loving approach.)

Believers have a way of majoring on the minors. In verses 16-17, Paul challenges the Roman church to refocus their attentions.

3. What should believers emphasize (v.17)? Practically speaking, what does this spiritual trifecta look like in the life of a believer?

4. What similar exhortation does Jesus give in Matthew 6:33?

To summarize the teaching of Jesus and Paul regarding the essentials of the faith, we should center our energies on the eternals instead of the externals.

5. In light of verses 18-19, think back over the last several weeks of our study in Romans and make a list of the non-negotiables, the spiritual essentials that Christians should prioritize in their lives.

When our freedom in Christ would hinder the spiritual growth of another believer, we must yield that liberty to the greater weight, love.

6. How would you summarize verses 20-23?

7. Read 1 Corinthians 10:23-24. In the space below, share a time when you have made a decision with respect to another believer, even though by "law" you could have done something different.

As we wrap up our study this week, take a few moments to consider Paul's closing words in Romans 14, "whatever is not from faith is sin." The Message phrases Romans 14:22-23 this way:

Cultivate your own relationship with God, but don't impose it on others. You're fortunate if your behavior and your belief are coherent. But if you're not sure, if you notice that you are acting in ways inconsistent with what you believe—some days trying to impose your opinions on others, other days just trying to please them—then you know that you're out of line. If the way you live isn't consistent with what you believe, then it's wrong.

On a daily basis, do you walk out what you believe? Are there areas of inconsistency (this is another word for sin) that you need to address? Record your commitment to obey God in those areas as a written prayer.

WEEK TEN

Others-Focused

Therefore, accept one another, just as Christ also accepted us to the glory of God.
Romans 15:7

In Romans 15, Paul continues his dialogue from Romans 14 regarding the way believers should relate to each other. Is it really possible for believers to live in unity without 100% conformity? Is uniformity the same thing as unity?

From the first day a young man or woman enters military service, the process of eliminating individuality begins. The method begins with the haircut and then proceeds to clothing. Service men and women all wear….that's right, uniforms. Every part of basic training is geared toward molding a group of individuals who previously functioned as sole components into a core of many who think and operate as one.

Some might think that this method could easily transfer to the body of Christ. However, Paul cautions those believers to take a different approach. There were three takeaways from this topic in Romans 14:

- Mature believers should not view weaker Christians with contempt.
- Weaker believers should not judge the liberty mature Christians have.
- Stronger Christians should not brandish their freedom in a way that would cause a younger brother or sister to stumble.

⫸ DAY ONE ⫷

Romans 15:1-7

1. In Romans 15:1, Paul classifies himself as a mature Christian. Read 1 Corinthians 9:12-22. What is his motivation for the way he relates to diverse people groups?

2. How does this same approach allow Paul to "bear the weaknesses" of less mature Christians? What is his motivation with them (v.2)?

In verses 1-2, Paul identifies the fundamental issue that threatens all relationships—selfishness.

3. What are some ways believers display selfishness in their relationships?

In verse 3, Paul quotes Psalm 69:9 and points his readers to the supreme example of selflessness, Jesus Christ.

4. Read Philippians 2:1-7 for a more detailed description of Christ's unselfish life. What did selflessness look like in his life?

5. In Philippians 2:19-21, Paul describes the selfless life of Timothy. Can you think of a believer you know who places the interests of others above his or her own? What is an example of selflessness from his or her life?

C. S. Lewis summarizes the principle of selflessness well:

> Give up yourself, and you will find your real self. Lose your life and you will save it. Submit to death, death of your ambitions and favorite wishes every day and the death of your whole body in the end: submit with every fiber of your being, and you will find eternal life. Keep back nothing. Nothing that you have not given away will be really yours. Nothing in you that has not died will ever be raised from the dead. Look for yourself, and you will find in the long run only hatred, loneliness, despair, rage, ruin, and decay. But look for Christ and you will find him, and with him everything else thrown in.[27]

6. What are the two sources of spiritual power that we can depend upon as we place others above ourselves (vv. 4-6)?

A note of caution is appropriate to emphasize at this point in our study. Although we are to choose to exercise love and "please our neighbor," we must be careful not to validate our neighbor's weakness. Giving in to weakness reduces the church to the lowest level of conscience in the body and does not urge weaker brothers and sisters to stretch and mature. Balance is the aim. We are to be considerate of our neighbors while at the same time challenge their thinking and perhaps, change their position.

7. What is the vital reason for unity among believers (Romans 15:7; John 17:20-26)?

⟫⟫ FILLING UP WITH FAITH

I do have rights…don't I?

Secular Humanism has pervaded American society for several decades, emphasizing the significance of self. This ideology is an affront to marriage, life, families, and every other institution created by God to bring glory to Him.

Speaking to the graduating class of Harvard University in 1978, Alexander Solzhenitsyn criticized rationalistic humanism and hedonism, noting that the emphasis on human rights rather than human responsibility was leading the American (and Western society) into "the abyss of human decadence."[28] Secular humanism espouses "autonomy of man from any higher authority above him."[29] This anthropocentric view regards man as the central element of existence rather than God. In another address in 1983, Solzhenitsyn noted:

> The social theories that promised so much have demonstrated their bankruptcy, leaving us at a dead end. The free people of the West could reasonably have been expected to realize that they are beset by numerous freely nurtured falsehoods, and not to allow lies to be foisted upon them so easily. All attempts to find a way out of the plight of today's world are fruitless unless we redirect our consciousness, in repentance, to the Creator of all: without this, no exit will be illumined, and we shall seek it in vain.[30]

What are some specific areas where Humanism is evident in the United States? What Biblical principle does acquiescing to that philosophy violate?

Area of Humanistic Influence	Biblical Principle Violated
A woman has the right to choose if she wants to keep or abort her unborn child.	Exodus 20:13; Jeremiah 1:5; Psalm 139:13-16; Job 31:15

Romans 15:8-24

As we discussed last week, the church in Rome was a hybrid group of believers. Jews and Gentiles. Slaves and masters. Rich and poor. Mature Christians and babes in Christ. What an interesting mix! In fact, the church at Rome had many similarities to the church today. As we read in Romans 14:1 and 15:7, accepting each other was an issue then, just as it is now. Acceptance is not just a mental activity. It is a practical outworking of our faith, faith in action. Accepting other believers is a matter of obedience; failing to do so is disobedience, plain and simple.

1. What are some practical ways that we can demonstrate acceptance and seek a common basis for fellowship with those who are different from us?

One of the key words we will see in the last two chapters of Romans is "ministry." Paul actually uses three Greek words to paint a more detailed picture for what he means:

"Ministry" in Romans 15-16

Greek Word	Translation	Verses Used
Diakonos	Servant, service, deacon	Romans 15:8, 25, 31; Romans 16:1
Leitourgos	Service in public office or the church	Romans 15:16, 27
Hierourgeo	To perform sacred rites or minister in priestly service	Romans 15:16

In our study today, we will examine two different ministries that exemplified acceptance: Jesus' ministry to the Gentiles (15:8-13) and Paul's ministry to the Gentiles (15:14-24).

Jesus is the ultimate example of a servant who inclusively ministered to all (See Luke 22:27). As we saw in Romans 1:16, His ministry on earth was directed to two groups, first the Jews and then the Gentiles. "To the Jew first" is a pattern that God established in the Old Testament, in the ministry of Christ, and in the early church. By God's design, the Good News was to be delivered to the Gentiles through the Jews.

2. In verses 9-12, Paul quotes four different Old Testament passages to demonstrate the blending of these two people groups. Summarize each passage to see a beautiful picture of God's plan.

Psalm 18:49 (Romans 15:9):

Deuteronomy 32:43 (Romans 15:10):

Psalm 117:1 (Romans 15:11):

Isaiah 11:10 (Romans 15:12):

3. Read Ephesians 2:12. How does Paul describe the pre-Christ life of the Gentiles?

4. By contrast, how does Paul describe the post-salvation life of the Gentiles (Romans 15:13)?

Beginning with verse 14, Paul transitions to a discussion of his personal ministry to the Gentiles. Up to this point in his letter, he has been writing *to* the church. Here, he begins to write *about* the believers in Rome.

5. Paul is convinced that three characteristics enable mature believers to have the spiritual capacity to help other believers mature. What are those three distinctions (v. 14)?

    •

    •

    •

6. Why was Paul able to speak out boldly to the believers in Rome, a church he had not founded (v. 15-16)?

Although he had a notable list of accomplishments on his resume, Paul made it clear in verses 17-21 that nothing he had done was through his own power or ability.

7. Quoting Isaiah 52:15, Paul shares his personal mission statement in verses 20-21 and in verse 22 explains that is the reason he has not been able to visit them. What is his compelling mission?

≫ FILLING UP WITH FAITH

Does the New Testament make the Old Testament obsolete?

Several times throughout the Book of Romans, Paul quotes passages from the Old Testament. Jesus also often quoted from the Old Testament (i.e. Genesis 1:27, Exodus 20:13, Deuteronomy 5:18, Deuteronomy 8:3, Isaiah 29:13, Isaiah 61:1-2, Hosea 6:6…) demonstrating the significance of the Old Testament. In fact, it was Jesus who said, "Do not think that I came to abolish the Law or the Prophets; I did not come to abolish but to fulfill" (Matthew 5:17). As we read in Romans 15:4, "whatever was written in earlier times was written for our instruction, so that through perseverance and the encouragement of the Scriptures we might have hope." In the Old Testament, we see the picture of God's love for his errant children unfolding in a beautiful way. In the New Testament, we see the fulfillment of God's plan for the salvation of mankind through the death and resurrection of His only Son. Both the Old Testament and the New Testament are God-breathed, inspired, and inerrant. Together, they are God's Word to us on how we should live.

Record at least one scripture from the Old Testament and the New Testament that have spoken to you through your time in God's Word this week. What did God say to you through the two passages?

Romans 15:25-33

Yesterday we looked at the way Jesus and Paul directed their ministry to the Gentiles. In today's passage, Paul writes about the way the Gentiles, having been the recipients of the ministry of grace, reached out in ministry to the Jews.

As Paul is writing his letter to the Roman believers, he had been in Corinth for about three months and is now headed to Jerusalem. He was travelling with a group of men who had been chosen by their churches in Macedonia (Philippi, Thessalonica, Berea) and Achaia to take offerings to the saints in Jerusalem and he wanted to use their generous example to encourage the church in Rome. Charles Swindoll notes, "The Gentile believers in Greece viewed their sharing of material wealth as a mere token of the debt they owed Jerusalem for the gift of the gospel, an immeasurable spiritual treasure."[31]

1. Why were the Gentile believers in Macedonia and Achaia "pleased" to give an offering to the church at Jerusalem (v. 27)?

In 2 Corinthians 8-9, Paul drills down to share the details about this offering. Although Paul does not state exactly what had precipitated the great need in Jerusalem, historians record a famine in the area so it is probable that a shortage of food was the issue.

2. Read 2 Corinthians 8:2-5. What was the socioeconomic status of the believers in the Macedonian churches? How does Paul describe the way they gave?

3. What is more important, the amount you give or the attitude with which you give (2 Corinthians 8:12-14)? How does Paul describe the attitude we should have in our giving?

4. Read Luke 21:1-4. How does widow's manner of giving apply to other areas of our lives such as our time and our talents?

In Romans 15:27, Paul explains that he viewed this offering as a repayment of a debt. The Gentiles had received their spiritual wealth from the Jews and they were reciprocating with a material gift. Paul's desire was that the offering would be a connecting point that would bind the Jews and Gentiles together.

In verses 30-33, Paul entreats the church in Rome to earnestly pray for him. The actual Greek word he uses is *sunagonisasthai* which means "to strive together with him." It was a word that was often used in association with a team sport where a group would put forth great effort to win.

5. What does *sunagonisasthai* prayer look like (v. 30)? The same word is used in Colossians 4:12 and is translated "laboring earnestly for you." Has there been a time when you strived with someone else in prayer, believing God for a victory? What was that like?

6. For what four specific needs did Paul ask them to join him in praying (v. 30-32)?

   •

   •

   •

   •

7. Paul closes this part of his letter with a common Jewish benediction. What blessing does he give to them (v. 33)?

In our study today, we saw that a famine had triggered suffering among the Jews in Jerusalem. In just a little more than a decade, we have seen the Gulf Coast ravaged by Hurricane Katrina, the Northeast devastated by Hurricane Sandy, and the small country of Haiti virtually wiped out by a substantial earthquake. These disasters have caused billions of dollars of damage and killed thousands. So the question could be asked:

Does God use natural catastrophes to punish people?

The following Old Testament incidents record some instances where God did use natural disasters for punishment. Read the verses below and record the catastrophic events that occurred.

I Kings 17:1, 7

Numbers 16:28-33

Exodus 7:14-21

Psalm 24:1 and 1 Corinthians 10:26 both confirm that God is sovereign over the universe. He is in control. However, that does not mean that every natural tragedy can be categorized as an "act of God."

Before the fall of man, the world was a perfect place. After Adam and Eve's rebellious sin, their separation from God changed the earth as they had known it. Records of earthquakes, floods, and drought pepper the pages of scripture. We live on an earth that has been cursed by sin. But, back to the question at hand—does God manipulate nature to punish people?

Read Matthew 5:45. Does God only visit disaster upon bad people?

This verse would seem to suggest that all natural catastrophes are not punishment. It is not that God cannot use such events for judgment, but according to Romans 8:22, sometimes "creation groans" and the laws of nature and physics are manifested.

Take a moment and reflect on the words of Deuteronomy 29:29. There are some answers that God just keeps to Himself. So perhaps the issue is not to wonder about the "secret things" but to ask ourselves, are we walking in obedience to all that He has revealed to us?

Romans 16:1-16

As we read our passage today, you will note that Paul extends greetings to a diverse group of 26 believers who were important to him and critical to his ministry. As you read, you will find that he sends salutations to rich, poor, men, women, prisoners, Romans, Greeks, and Jews.

1. What does the Bible say about diversity in the body of Christ?

    Galatians 3:28

    Colossians 3:11

    Revelation 7:9-10

2. For the sake of our study today, let's take a few minutes and focus on the ten women that Paul mentions and make notes on what we learn about them.

    Phoebe (vv. 1-2)

    • Most theologians believe that the reason Paul is writing this recommendation for Phoebe is because she was delivering his letter to the church in Rome.

    Priscilla (vv. 3-5; Acts 18:2-3, 18-19, 26; 2 Timothy 4:19)

    Mary (v. 6)

    Junia (v. 7)

    Tryphena and Tryphosa (v. 12)

    • Most commentators think these two were sisters and perhaps twins due to similarities in their names.

Persis (v. 12)

Rufus's mother (v. 13)

Julia and Nereus' sister (v. 15)

3.   In verse 5, Paul also sends a special greeting to Epaenetus. Why is this man so dear to Paul?

Paul shared Jesus with people everywhere he went. Evangelism was in his DNA. He didn't have to think about it or set aside a special visitation time every week, sharing Jesus was the natural outflow of his daily life.

4.   What about you? Have you shared Christ with anyone this week? What was your experience like?

5.   Summarize what you learned about the early church as you read this passage today.

1 Peter 3:15 challenges us "to always being ready to make a defense to everyone who asks you to give an account for the hope that is in you." Today, Paul gave testimony to leading Epaenetus to Christ.

How would you answer an unbeliever who asked you, like the jailer asked Paul and Silas,

What must I do to be saved (Acts 16:30)?

First, be ready to share your own salvation experience.

Write a brief 5-7 sentence salvation testimony in the space below. A great outline to follow is my life before Christ, how I received Christ, my life since I received Christ.

Second, have a scriptural gospel presentation committed to memory. Your presentation can be as simple as sharing these three verses:

Romans 3:23 - *For all have sinned and fall short of the glory of God.*

Romans 6:23 - *For the wages of sin is death, but the free gift of God is eternal life in Christ Jesus our Lord.*

Romans 10:13 – *For whoever will call on the name of the Lord will be saved.*

Romans 16:17-27

In Paul's final instructions to the church at Rome, he once again, shifts his attention to the subject of unity. Dissension is one of the weapons Satan commonly uses to distract and discourage believers. Disunity is dangerous, draining, and destructive. In this particular instance, Paul is warning the believers in Rome to avoid false teachers who cause dissension by deceiving "the hearts of the unsuspecting" (v. 18).

1. To what are false teachers enslaved? What devices do they use in their deception (v. 18)?

Typically, false teachers incorporate just enough of the truth in their message to lure their victims into a carefully constructed trap of lies. In verse 19, Paul praises the believers in Rome for their obedience, but he also encourages them to be discerning and biblically sound so that false teachers will not mislead them.

2. Read Acts 17:10-12. What was the daily practice of the Berean believers (v.11)?

3. Take a moment to reflect on Acts 17:10-12. If Paul were writing this commendation today, could he use you as an example of being more "noble minded"?

The phrase Paul uses in Romans 16:20 is similar to God's pronouncement in Genesis 3:15 when he says that the seed of woman will bruise the head of the serpent. In contrast to the God of peace, false teachers/preachers breed discord and confusion.

In Romans 16:21, Paul sends the church greetings from a number of men who were travelling with him, including Timothy, his disciple in ministry.

4. Jesus had disciples. Paul had disciples. Do you? Who are you investing your life in? Making disciples is a command (Matthew 28:18-20). Are you walking in obedience in this area of your life?

5. In Romans 16:25, how does Paul describe the work of Christ in the life of a believer?

As Paul concludes his letter to the Romans, you can almost hear the excitement in his voice (remember he dictated his letters) as he explains the way God's plan for the Gentiles is coming into being. Read Romans 16:25-27 in The Message:

> *All of our praise rises to the One who is strong enough to make you strong, exactly as preached in Jesus Christ, precisely as revealed in the mystery kept secret for so long but now an open book through the prophetic Scriptures. All the nations of the world can now know the truth and be brought into obedient belief, carrying out the orders of God, who got all this started, down to the very last letter. All our praise is focused through Jesus on this incomparably wise God! Yes!*

As we come to the end of our time in Romans, take some time to consider the ways God has moved in your life in these ten weeks.

PRAYERS GOD HAS ANSWERED

HOW GOD HAS SPOKEN TO ME THROUGH HIS WORD

OPPORTUNITIES I HAVE HAD TO ENGAGE UNBELIEVERS WITH THE TRUTH

Dear one, has there ever been a time that you have given your heart to the Lord? Do you have the assurance that if you were to die right now, you would go straight to heaven to spend all eternity in the presence of the Lord Jesus Christ and all His followers? If not, please let me share with you how you can be saved.

Admit Your Sin

First, you must understand that you are a sinner. The Bible says, *All have sinned and fall short of the glory of God* (Rom. 3:23). In Romans 6:23 the Bible says, *For the wages of sin is death.* That means that sin has separated us from a Holy God and we are under the sentence of eternal death and separation from God.

Abandon Self-Effort

Secondly, you must understand that you cannot save yourself by your own efforts. The Bible is very clear that it is *not by works of righteousness which we have done, but according to His mercy He saved us* (Titus 3:5). Again, in Ephesians 2:8-9 the Bible says, *For by grace you have been saved through faith; and that not of yourselves, it is the gift of God; not as a result of works, that no one should boast.*

Acknowledge Christ's Payment

Thirdly, you must believe that Jesus Christ, the Son of God, died for your sins. The Bible says, *God demonstrates His own love toward us, in that while we were yet sinners, Christ died for us* (Rom. 5:8). That means He died a sacrificial death in your place. Your sin debt has been paid by the blood of Jesus Christ, which *cleanses us from all sin* (I John 1:7).

Accept Him as Savior

Fourthly, you must put your faith in Jesus Christ and Him alone for your salvation. The blood of Christ does you no good until you receive Him by faith. The Bible says, *Believe on the Lord Jesus Christ, and you shall be saved* (Acts 16:31).

Has there been a time in your life that you have taken this all-important step of faith? If not, I urge you to do it right now. Jesus Christ is the only way to heaven. He said, *"I am the way, the truth, and the life; no man comes unto the Father, but by Me"* (John 14:16).

Would you like to become a Christian? Would you like to invite Jesus Christ to come into your heart today? Read over this prayer and if it expresses the desire of your heart, you may ask Him into your heart to take away your sin, fill you with His Spirit, and take you to home to heaven when you die. If this is your intention, pray this prayer.

"Oh God, I'm a sinner. I am lost and I need to be saved. I know I cannot save myself, so right now, once and for all, I trust You to save me. Come into my heart, forgive my sin, and make me Your child. I give you my life. I will live for You as You give me Your strength. Amen"

If you will make this your heartfelt prayer, God will hear and save you! Jesus has promised that He will never leave nor forsake anyone who comes to Him in faith. In John 6:37 He said, *"The One who comes to Me I will certainly not cast out."*

(2008). *The ESV Study Bible*. Wheaton, IL: Crossway.

Easton, M. (1996). *Easton's Bible Dictionary*. Oak Harbor, WA: Logos Research Systems, Inc.

Geisler, N.L. (2012). *The Big Book of Christian Apologetics*. Grand Rapids, MI: Baker Books.

Gunter, S. (1995). *Prayer Portions*. Birmingham, AL: The Fathers Business.

Lewis, C. S. (1960). *Mere Christianity*. New York, NY: Macmillan Publishing.

McDowell, J. & McDowell, S. (2012). *77 FAQs About God and the Bible*. Eugene, OR: Harvest House Publishers.

McGee, J. M. (1991). *Thru the Bible Commentary Series: Romans 1-8*. Nashville, TN: Thomas Nelson Publishers.

McGee, R. (1990). *The Search for Significance*. Houston, TX: Rapha Publishing.

Meiderlen, P. Quoted in Barton, B., Veerman, D. & Wilson, N. (1992). Romans. In G. Osborne (Ed.),
   Life Application Commentary. Carol Stream, IL: Tyndale House Publishers, Inc.

Phillips, J. A. (1969). *Exploring Romans*. Chicago, IL: Moody Press.

Sharp, M. J. (2012). *Defending the Faith*. Grand Rapids, MI: Kregel Publications.

Solzhenitsyn, A. (1978). *A World Split Apart: Commencement Address at Harvard University*.
   http://www.americanrhetoric.com/speeches/alexandersolzhenitsynharvard.htm.

Solzhenitsyn, A. (1983). *Men Have Forgotten God: The Templeton Address*.
   http://www.roca.org/OA/36/36h.htm.

Strobel, L. (2000). *The Case for Faith*. Grand Rapids, MI: Zondervan.

Subjection. (n.d.) *American Heritage® Dictionary of the English Language, Fifth Edition*.
   (2011). Retrieved November 15 2016 from http://www.thefreedictionary.com/subjection.

Swindoll, C. (2015). *Insights on Romans*. Carol Stream, IL: Tyndale House Publishers, Inc.

Tackett, D. *What's a Christian Worldview?* www.focusonthefamily.com/faith/christian-worldview.

Walvoord, J.F., Zuck, R. B. & Dallas Theological Seminary. (1985). *The Bible Knowledge Commentary: An Exposition
   of the Scriptures* (vol. 2). Wheaton, IL: Victor Books.

Wiersbe, W. (1989). *The Bible Exposition Commentary*. Wheaton, IL: Victor Books.

Williams, S. (2009). *Real Faith*. Colllierville, TN: Instant Publishers.

Zacharias, R. & Geisler, N. (2003). *Who Made God?*. Grand Rapids, MI: Zondervan.

WEEK 1

1. Easton, M. (1996). *Easton's Bible Dictionary*. Oak Harbor, WA: Logos Research Systems, Inc.

2. Walvoord, J.F., Zuck, R. B. & Dallas Theological Seminary. (1985). *The Bible Knowledge Commentary: An Exposition of the Scriptures* (vol. 2, p. 436). Wheaton, IL: Victor Books.

3. McGee, J. M. (1991). *Thru the Bible Commentary Series: Romans 1-8*, p. 20. Nashville, TN: Thomas Nelson Publishers.

4. McGee, J. M. (1991). *Thru the Bible Commentary Series: Romans 1-8*, p. 24. Nashville, TN: Thomas Nelson Publishers.

5. Geisler, N.L. (2012). *The Big Book of Christian Apologetics*, p. 490-491, Grand Rapids, MI: Baker Books.

6. Williams, S. (2009). *Real Faith*, p. 64. Colllierville, TN: Instant Publishers.

7. Geisler, N.L. (2012). *The Big Book of Christian Apologetics*, p. 13, Grand Rapids, MI: Baker Books.

8. Phillips, J. A. (1969). *Exploring Romans*. Chicago, IL: Moody Press.

WEEK 3

9. Geisler, N.L. (2012). *The Big Book of Christian Apologetics*, p. 505. Grand Rapids, MI: Baker Books.

WEEK 7

10. Wiersbe, W. (1989). *The Bible Exposition Commentary*, p. 546. Wheaton, IL: Victor Books.

11. Zacharias, R. & Geisler, N. (2003). *Who Made God?*, p. 31. Grand Rapids, MI: Zondervan.

12. McDowell, J. & McDowell, S. (2012). *77 FAQs About God and the Bible*, p. 111. Eugene, OR: Harvest House Publishers.

13. Strobel, L. (2000). *The Case for Faith*, p. 146. Grand Rapids, MI: Zondervan.

14. (2008). *The ESV Study Bible*, p. 2509. Wheaton, IL: Crossway.

15. (2008). *The ESV Study Bible*, p. 2510. Wheaton, IL: Crossway.

16. Sharp, M. J. (2012). *Defending the Faith*, p. 55. Grand Rapids, MI: Kregel Publications.

WEEK 8

17. McDowell, J. & McDowell, S. (2012). *77 FAQs About God and the Bible*, p. 128. Eugene, OR: Harvest House Publishers.

18. McGee, R. (1990). *The Search for Significance*, p. 140. Houston, TX: Rapha Publishing.

19. McGee, R. (1990). *The Search for Significance*, p. 141. Houston, TX: Rapha Publishing.

20. Tackett, D. *What's a Christian Worldview?* www.focusonthefamily.com/faith/christian-worldview.

21. McDowell, J. & McDowell, S. (2012). *77 FAQs About God and the Bible*, p. 46. Eugene, OR: Harvest House Publishers.

22. McDowell, J. & McDowell, S. (2012). *77 FAQs About God and the Bible*, p. 51. Eugene, OR: Harvest House Publishers.

WEEK 9

23. Subjection. (n.d.) *American Heritage® Dictionary of the English Language, Fifth Edition*. (2011). Retrieved November 15 2016 from http://www.thefreedictionary.com/subjection

24. Lewis, C. S. (1960). *Mere Christianity*, p. 116. New York, NY: Macmillan Publishing.

25. Meiderlen, P. Quoted in Barton, B., Veerman, D. & Wilson, N. (1992). Romans. In G. Osborne (Ed.), *Life Application Commentary*, p. 250. Carol Stream, IL: Tyndale House Publishers, Inc.

WEEK 10

26. Lewis, C.S. (1960). *Mere Christianity*, p. 190. New York, NY: Macmillan Publishing.
27. Solzhenitsyn, A. (1978). *A World Split Apart: Commencement Address at Harvard University*. http://www.americanrhetoric.com/speeches/alexandersolzhenitsynharvard.htm
28. Ibid.
29. Solzhenitsyn, A. (1983). *Men Have Forgotten God*: The Templeton Address. http://www.roca.org/OA/36/36h.htm
30. Swindoll, C. (2015). *Insights on Romans*, p. 355. Carol Stream, IL: Tyndale House Publishers, Inc.

# NOTES

NOTES

Made in the USA
Lexington, KY
12 January 2017